I0751612

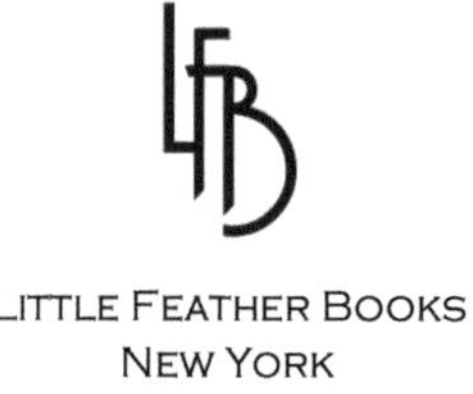

LITTLE FEATHER BOOKS
NEW YORK

the Karma of a Woman

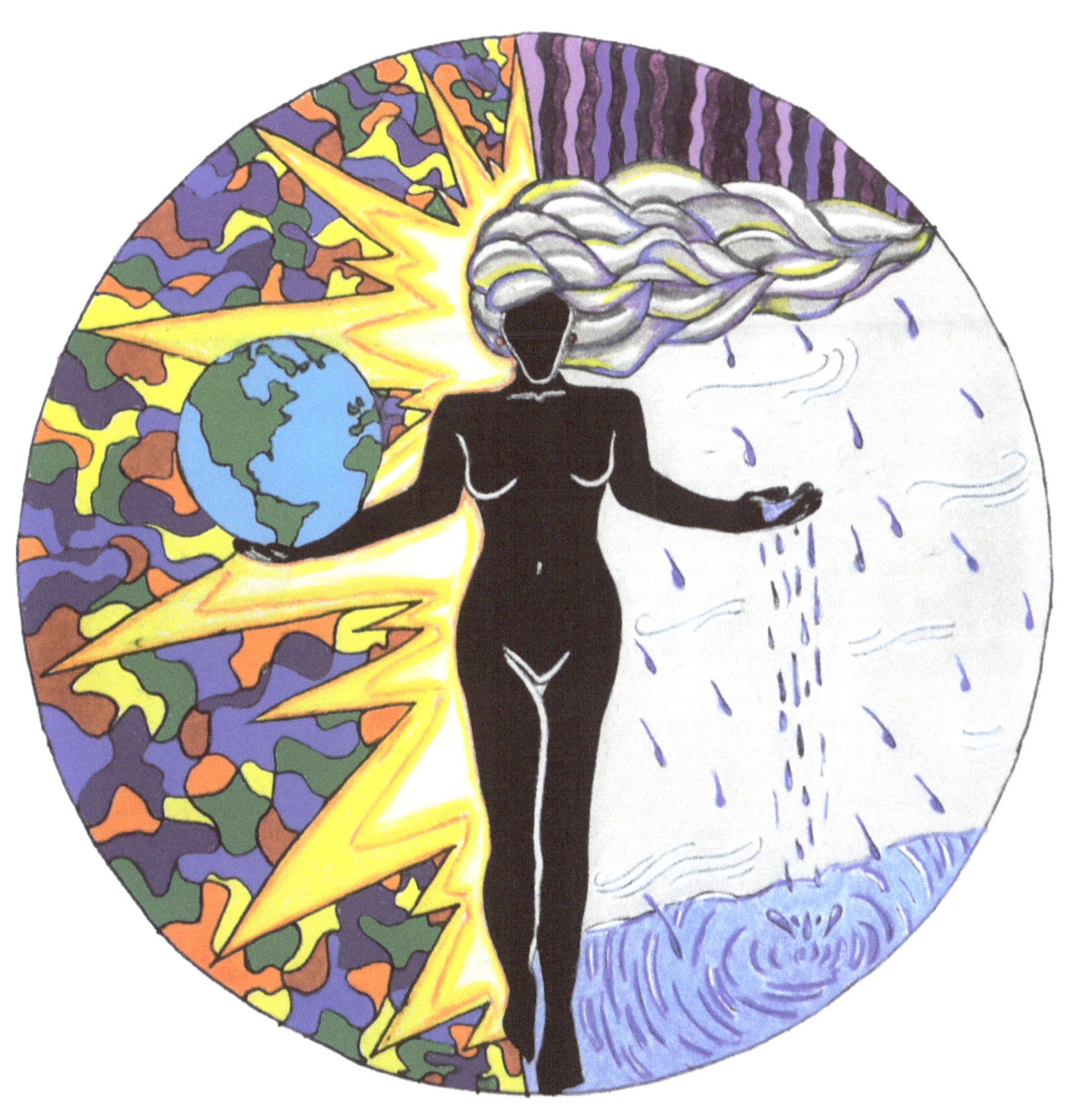

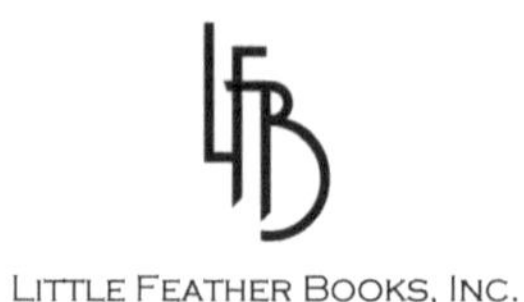

Little Feather Books, Inc.

Library of Congress Cataloging-in-Publication data on file.
ISBN: 978-0-9907790-3-2

Dedication

This book is dedicated to the women who chose not to physically meet their children.
You are not alone in this world.

To my own unborn children, may our souls both find peace and forgiveness.

—Barbara Pierson

I dedicate my mandalas to all of the women who were, are, and will continue to be.
May you remember that your power lies in you.

—Kimberly Febo

About Mandalas

I came across the teachings of the mandala "by chance," and since then, I have not been the same person.

Throughout my life, I've suffered from anxiety and periods of depression. After a while I had become so overwhelmed with these recurring feelings, that I reached a point where I knew something had to give before I completely lost it. In stumbling upon this form of art I soon discovered that I had been blessed with the gift to draw and create my own mandalas, whether for my own therapy or for others.

The contents within the circle of a mandala contain the essence that is within you at the moment of creation. Within this essence lay the tools that you are seeking to continue throughout your life's journey. For the observer, it is a guide that another human being provides to give you clues to help find yourself by journeying inward. In studying, analyzing, and meditating on each piece, you are consciously and subconsciously letting your mind, heart, and spirit translate what you are seeing while simultaneously allowing yourself to be a witness and a student to your inner self. To me, this experience is the ultimate practice of helping to heal oneself as well as one another. I feel driven to share my work with mandalas with the rest of the world in any way I can, and truly believe this form of art can continue to greatly impact the people who come across it through their own search and enjoyment.

The word mandala (man-DAH-lah) comes from the classical Indian language of Sanskrit and literally means "circle" or "center." Broken down, it is derived from the root "manda," which means essence, to which the suffix "la," meaning container, has been added. Thus, one obvious connotation of mandala is that it is a container of essence.

Mandalas may capture a moment in time, just like a photo, and embody it as a circular picture or object. The circle is a potent and universal symbol of wholeness and eternity; hence, a circle never ends. They may also be used as a picture to tell a story, beautifully representing both the visible world outside of us (the circle) and the invisible world deep inside our mind, body, and soul (the center).

Mandalas are considered to be one of the oldest forms of art and have been used throughout the world for self-expression, spiritual transformation, and personal growth. The symbols and visual images inscribed in a mandala vary from culture to culture. Many are designed intricately using extreme geometrical detail with colors and shapes creating a symmetrical picture within the circle. Some traditions portray pictures of gods, goddesses and other natural objects. The Tibetans viewed the mandala as symbolic diagram of the greater cosmos, and Native Americans used them in healing rituals. Even in Christian cathedrals, the labyrinth is a mandalic pattern used as a tool for meditation.

Regardless of what part of the world they are used, mandalas transcend all religions, they speak the language of spirit. They are so powerful they have even been applied in more recent years as scientific tools of psychotherapy. Swiss psychologist Carl Jung developed the use of mandalas as an aid to psychological understanding. Jung came to see the mandala as a pathway to the self, and he began to use them in his work as a psychiatrist to help his patients make deeper connections with themselves. His idea was that entering the circle or sphere of the mandala represented the psyche that holds within it, at the center, the true self. Today, mandala drawing and coloring has become a widely practiced form of art-therapy, relaxation and hypnosis.

There are many natural mandala forms to be found all around us. We see them in celestial circles, such as the earth, moon, sun, and constellations. Artistically, they can be conveyed as conceptual circles, such as family, friends, and communities. We see them even in clothing designs, logos, and emblems. They are everywhere! And the beauty of it all is that, once they are brought to your awareness, it is difficult not to spot them.

No matter the type of mandala, each one contains its own wisdom and truth. To unlock its secrets, we must look past the first superficial impression, appreciate the detail within each tiny aspect of the pattern, and allow every detail to surface, allowing thoughts and feelings to surface as well. No matter how positive or negative the feelings may be. The mandala helps you to surface them and show you what is going on within your inner being. All you have to do is listen.

So, allow the mandalas in this story to speak to you. As you observe them, do not push back or shun any thoughts or feelings that may come to light. Be brave enough to listen to what your inner essence is telling you. Dare to come up with your own conclusion by viewing them and being a part of the journey that we are all a part of. In understanding the potential messages of each symbol, shape, or color and what they mean to you, something inside will draw you closer to a place of centeredness and peace. This intricate way of seeing, of always looking more deeply into things, brings forth an original and fresh way of experiencing the world around us. There is always more to see, as is such with mandalas.

—Kimberly Febo, Illustrator

the Karma of a Woman

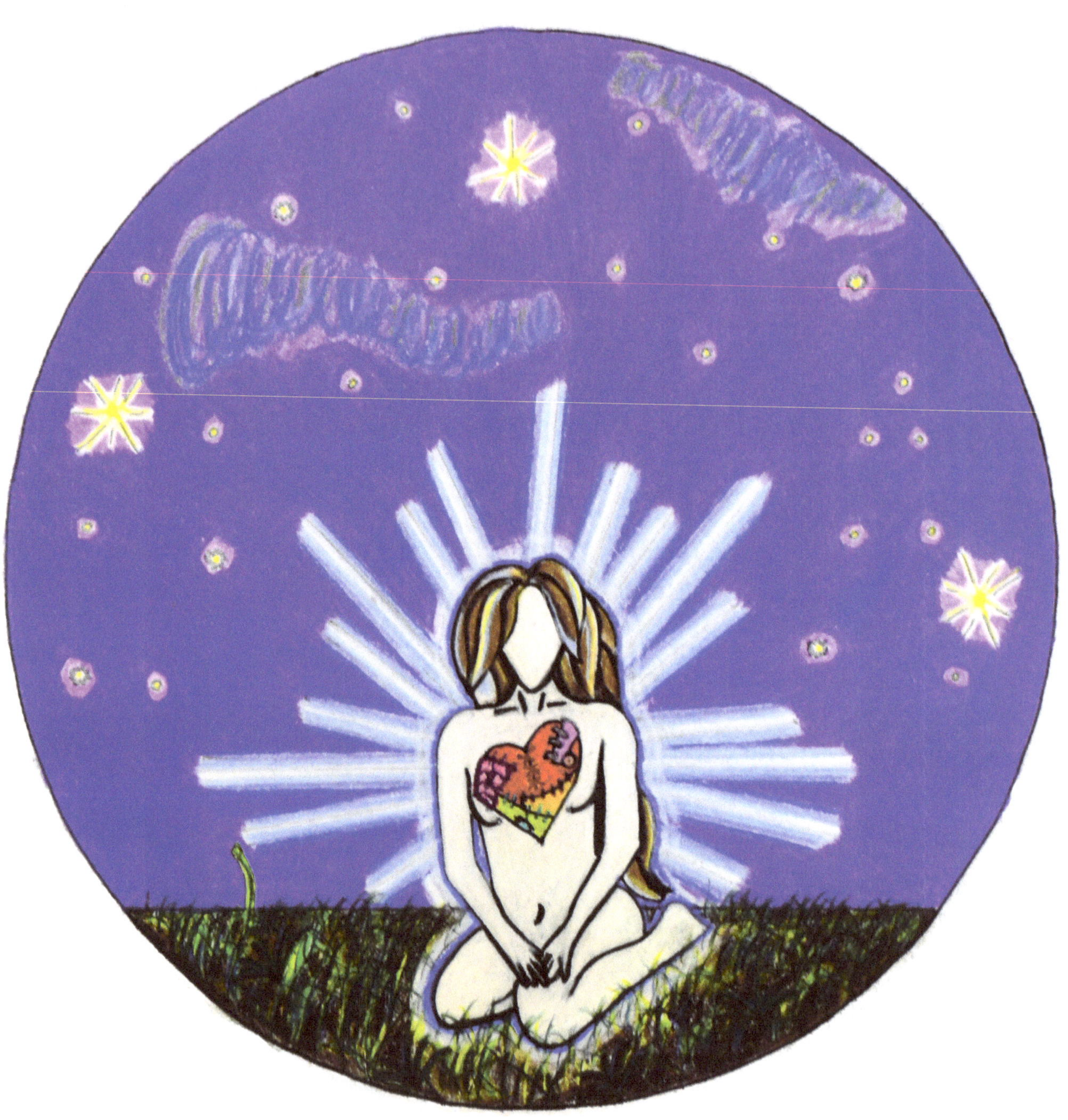

Her heart weathered and wise from experience

Yet still, with all the love of the universe in Her soul

She remains a beautiful light

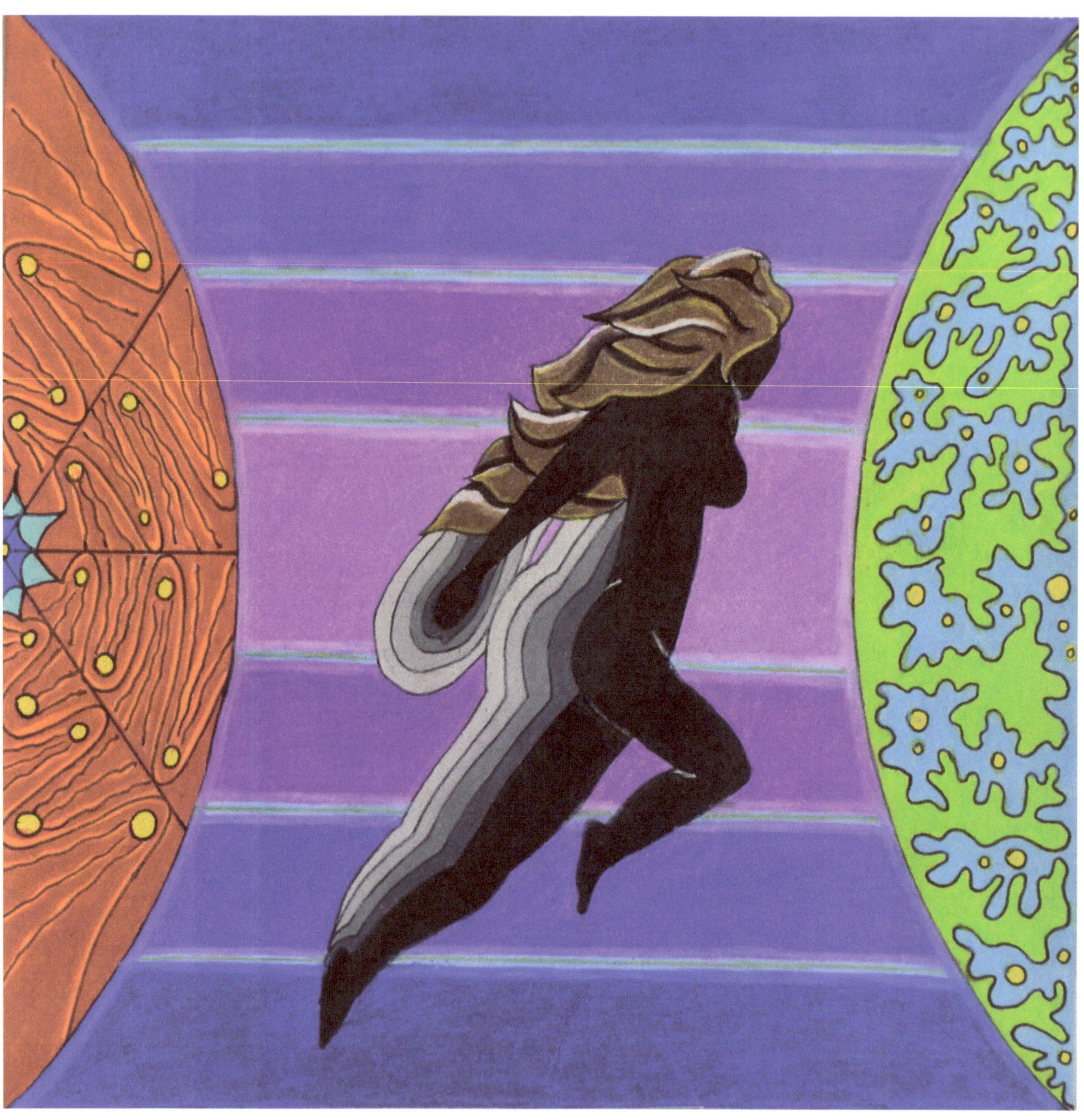

Traveling from body to body,

Lifetime through lifetime

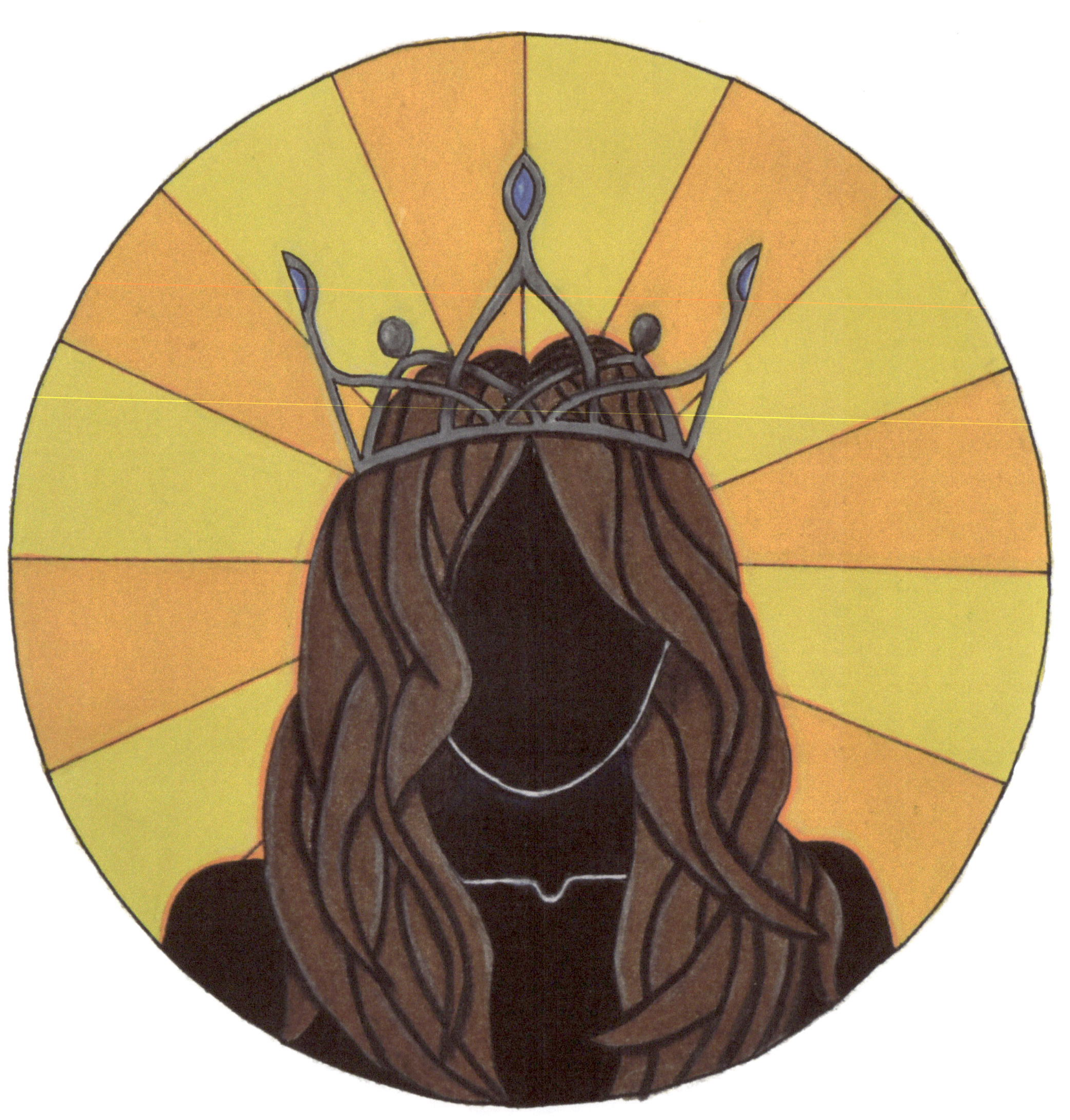

Wearing Her crown

Always shining

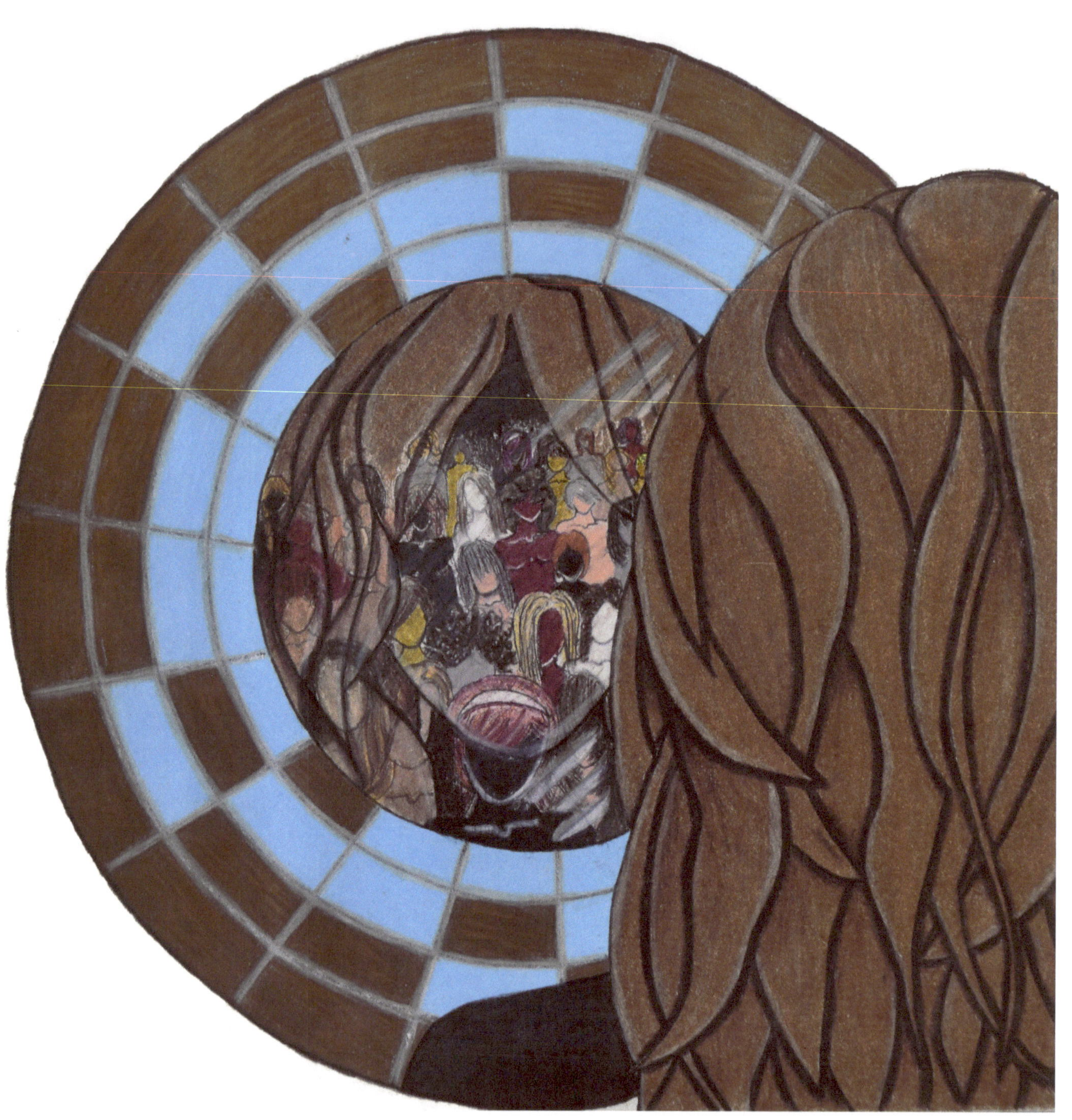

You can see it in Her eyes
when She looks at you

Her eyes are your own.

Full of what is past
Full of unconditional love, curiosity, innocence

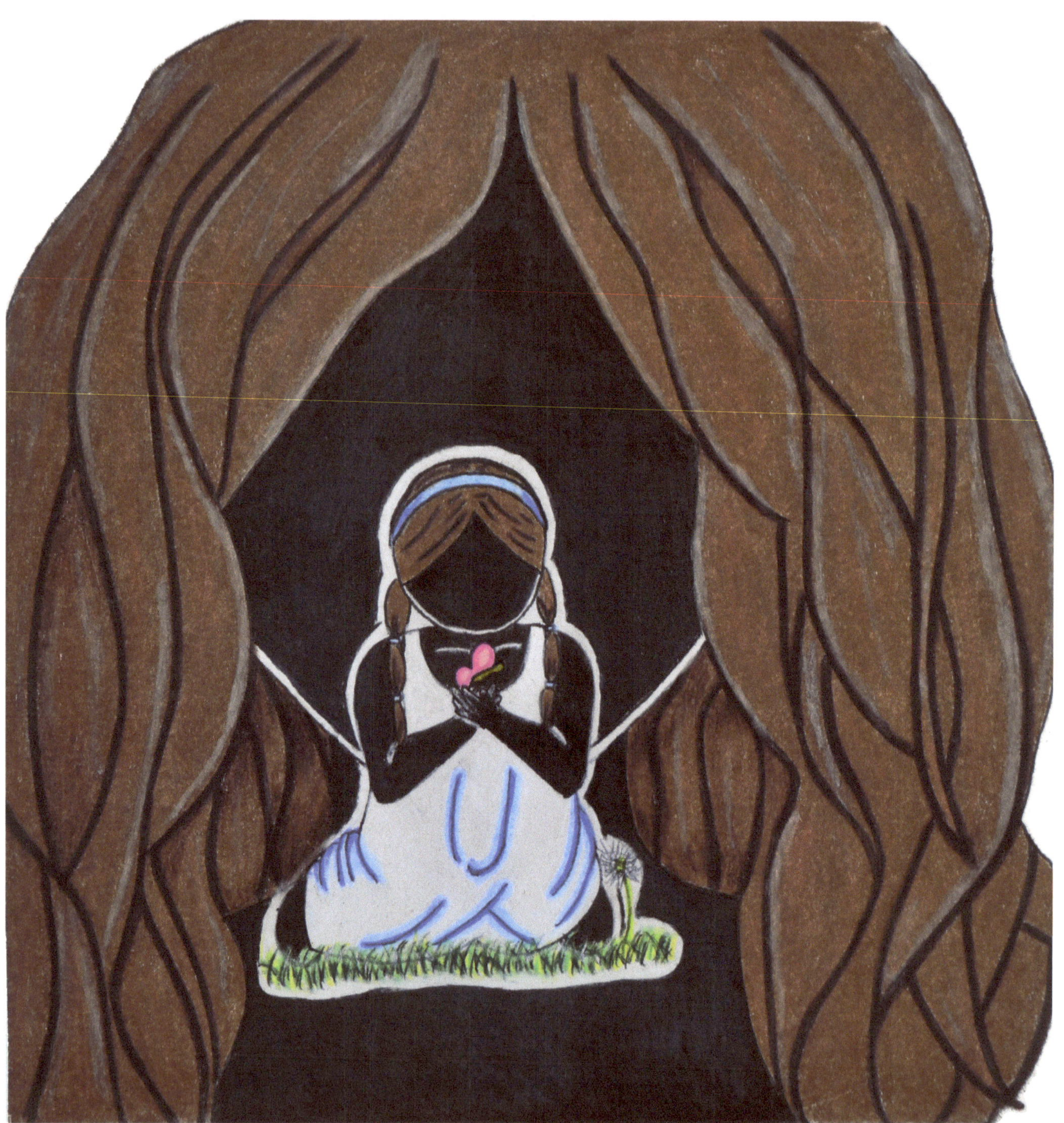

Like the child within Her.

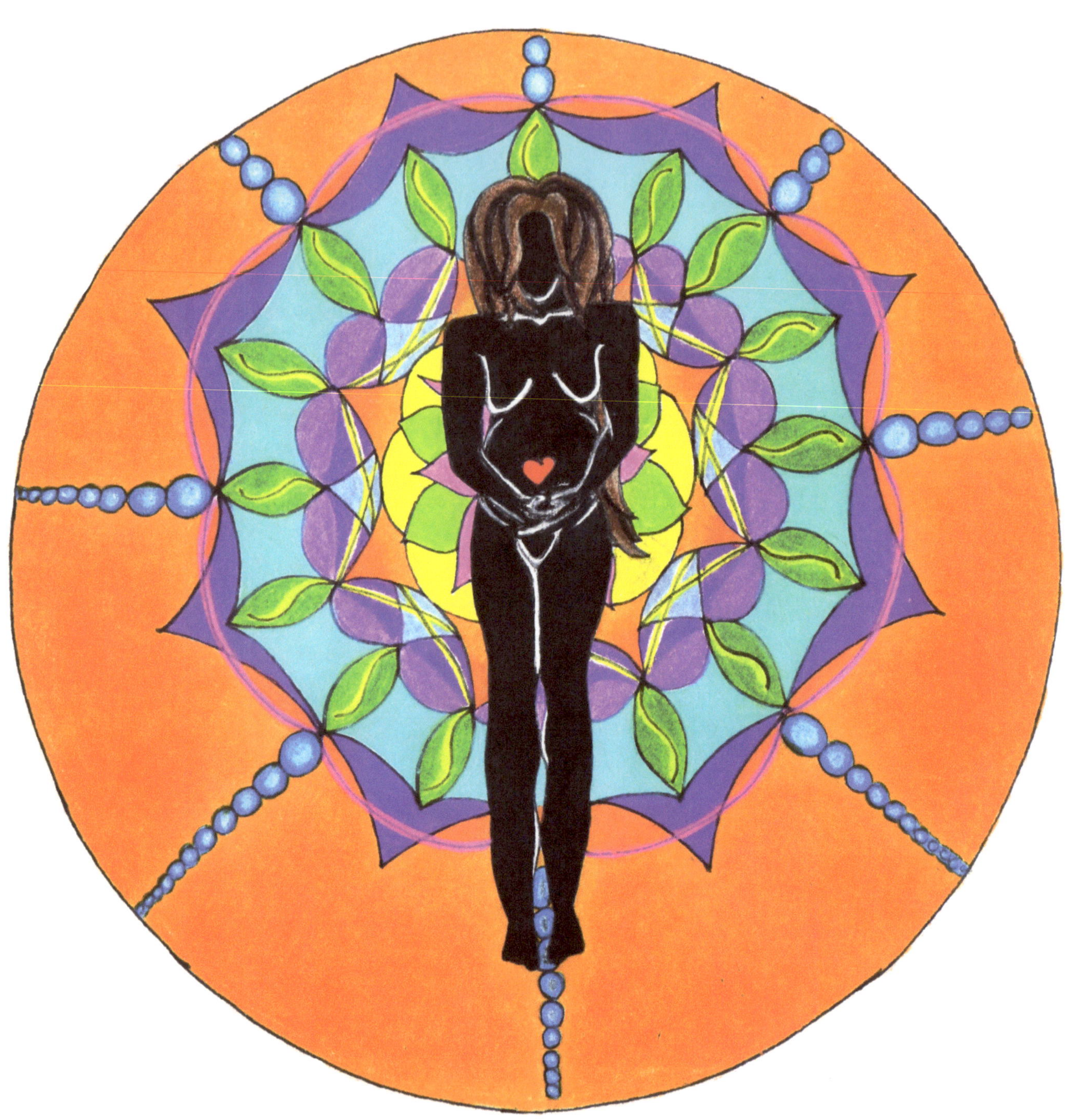

...Like the child

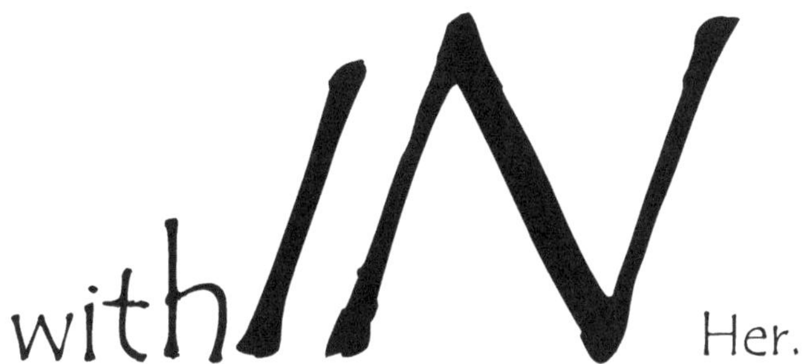

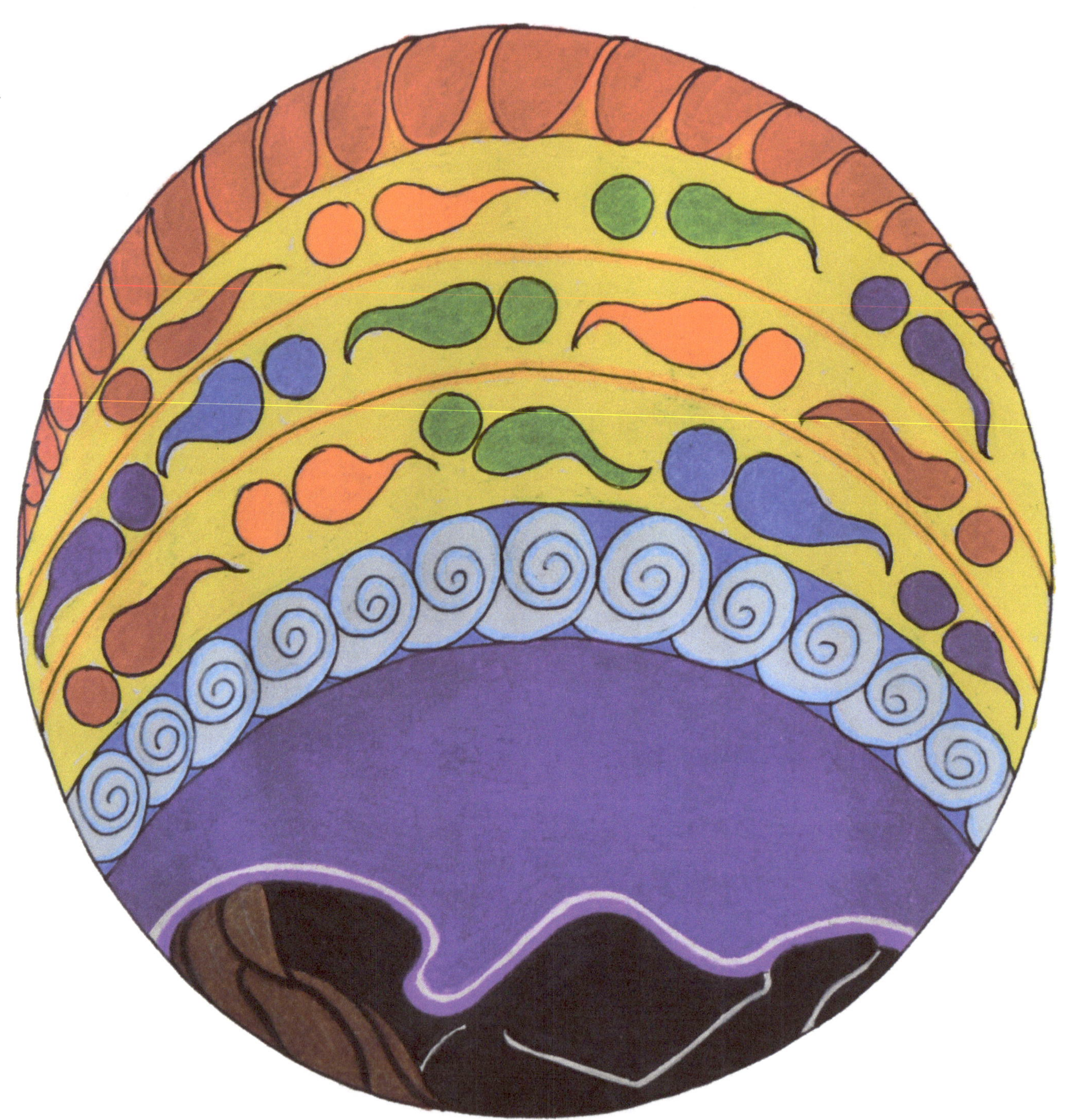

Previous lives filled with the
joys and pains of motherhood

She hears the sounds of Her children
in far off dimensions

Light years beyond this physical existence.

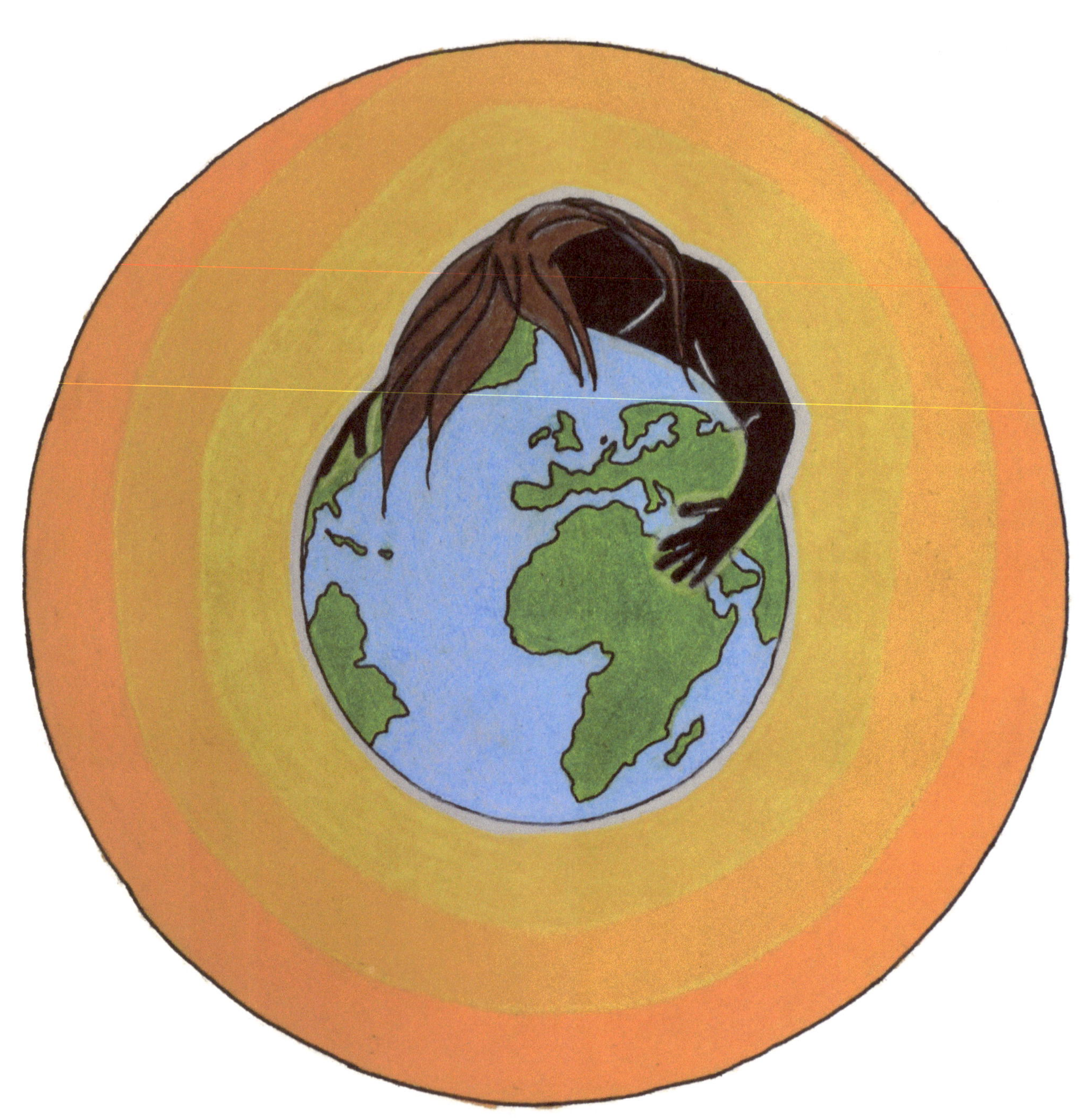

She gives Herself to others

the only way She knows how

Passionately. Maternally.

Instinct.

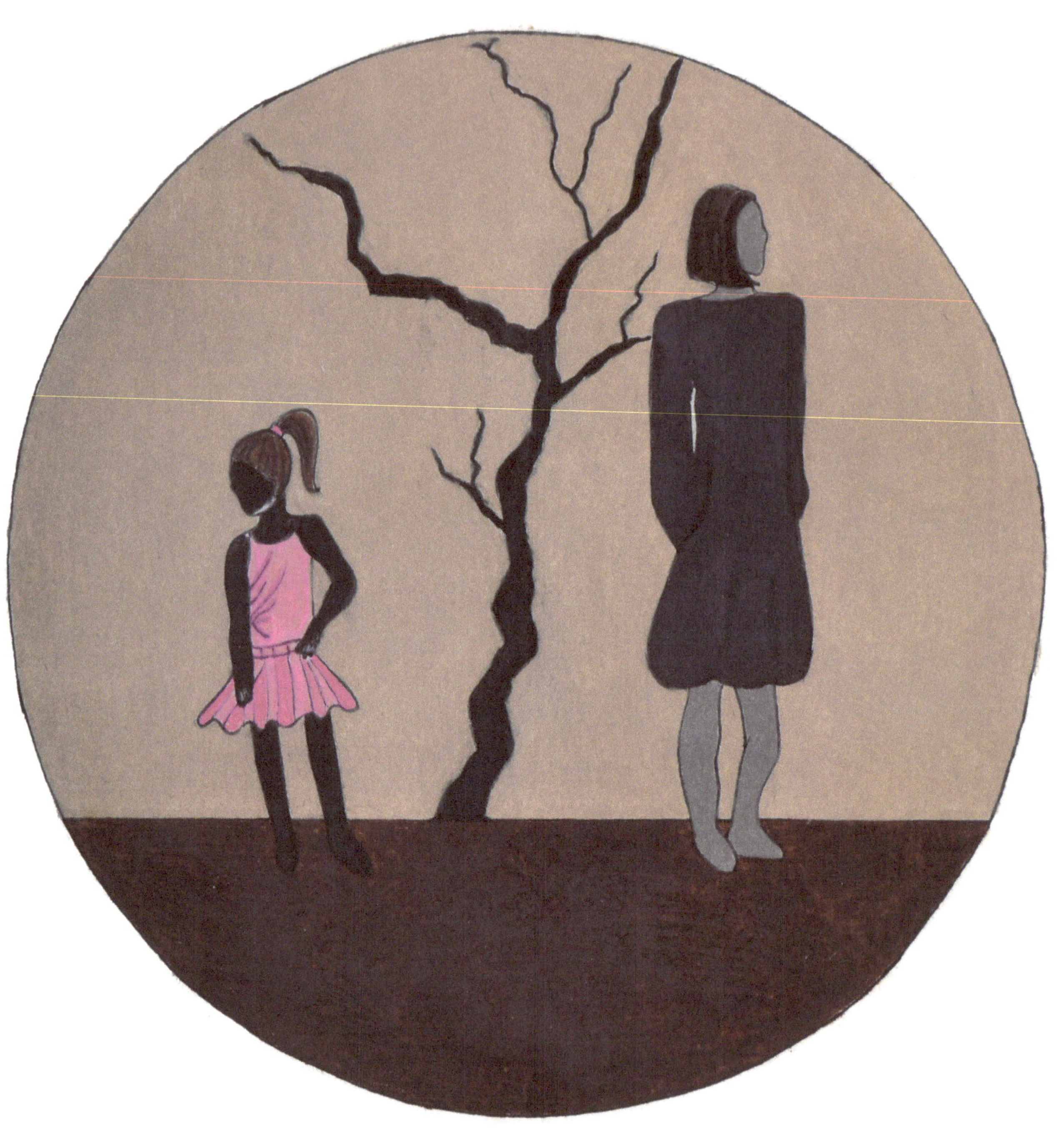

Not learned from Her own mother, no.

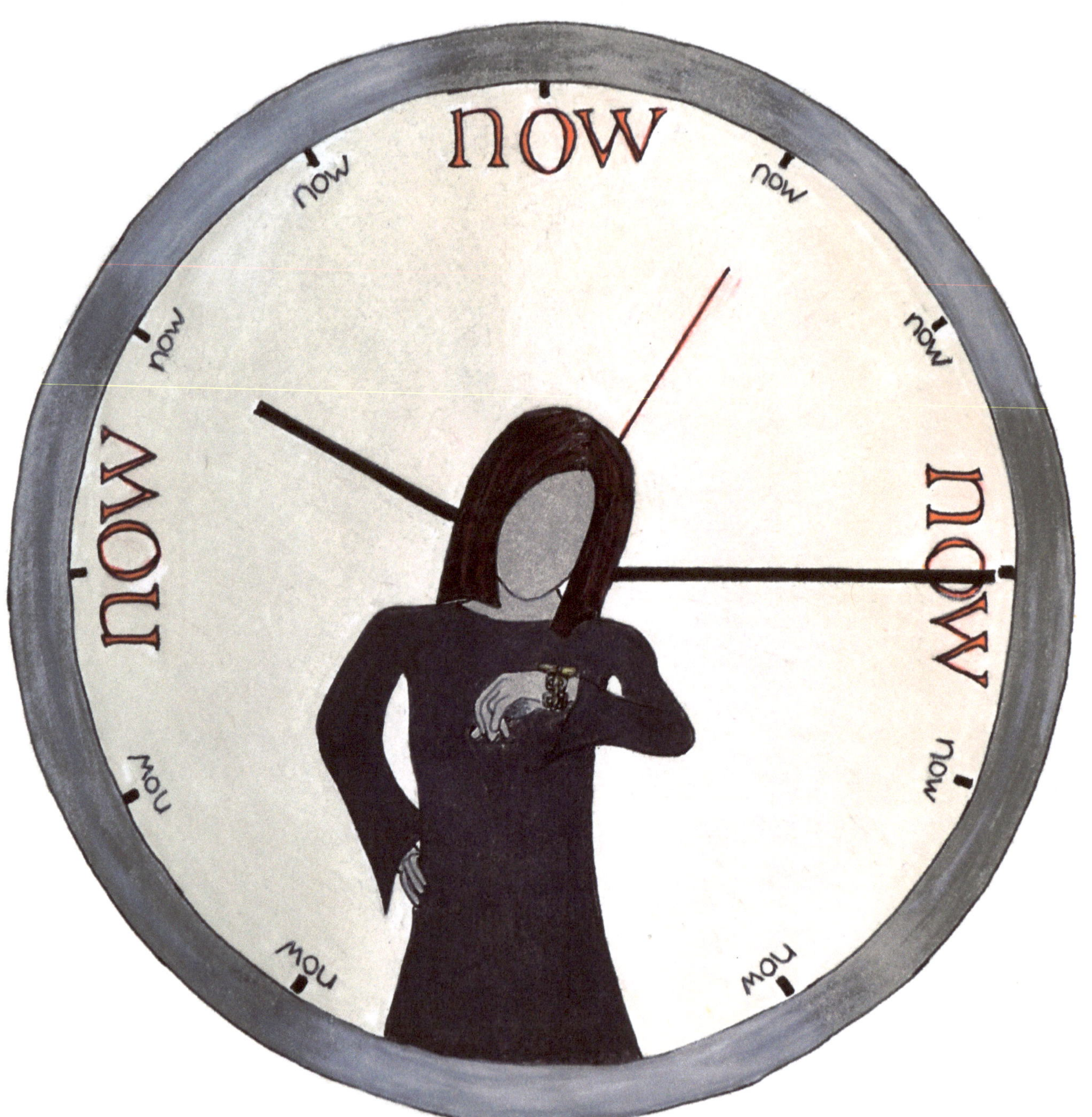
now
now
now
now
now
now
now
now
now
now
now
now

Her own mother,

Fixated on HOW and WHEN

to love her daughter

Rather than just TO love her daughter

No, no.

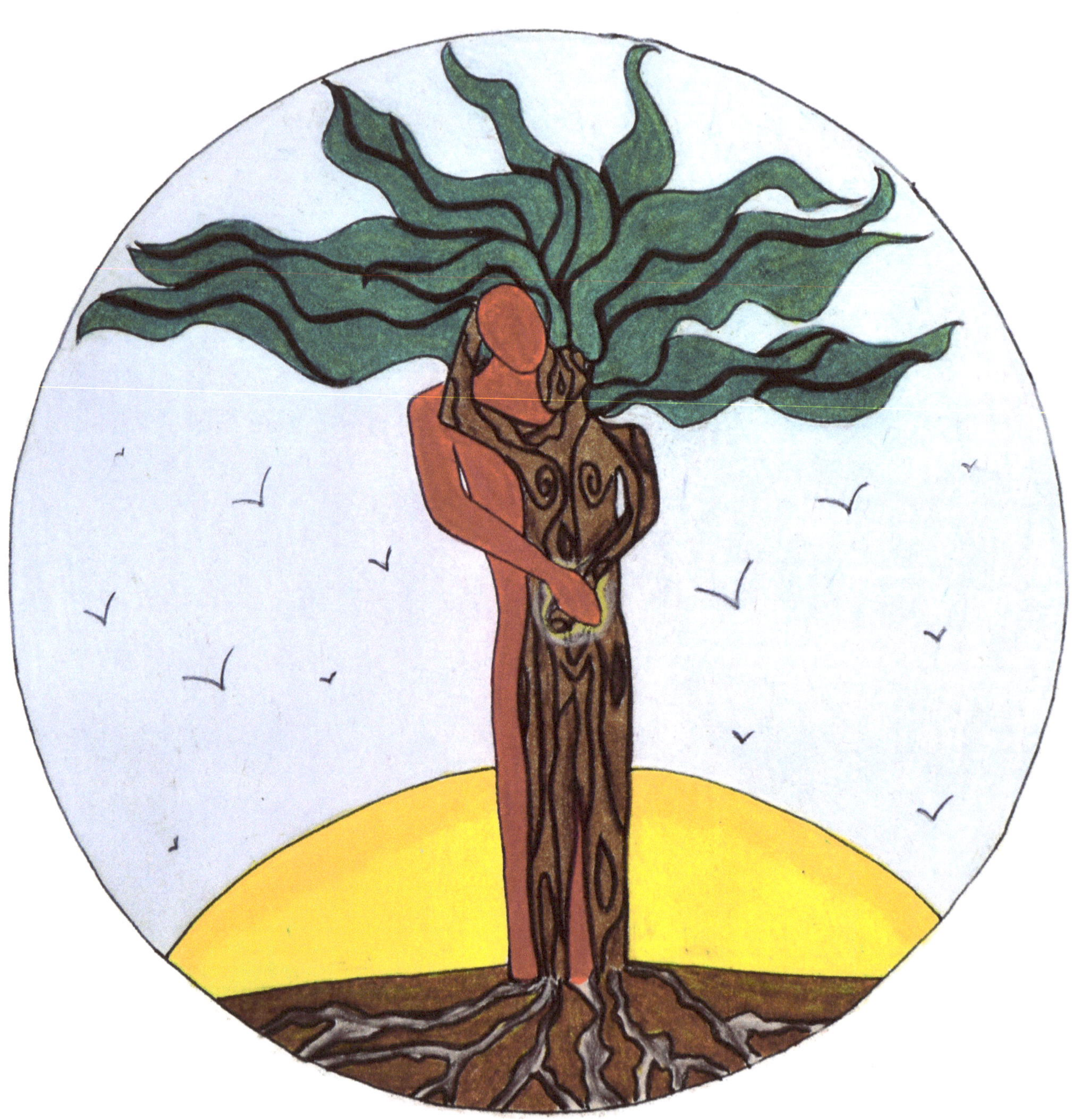

Her own instinct.

A woman powerful and aware of Herself
and her goddess-given rights

The right to live, to love, to grow
To do whatever the fuck She wants
Whoever the *fuck* She wants
Whenever the **FUCK** She wants

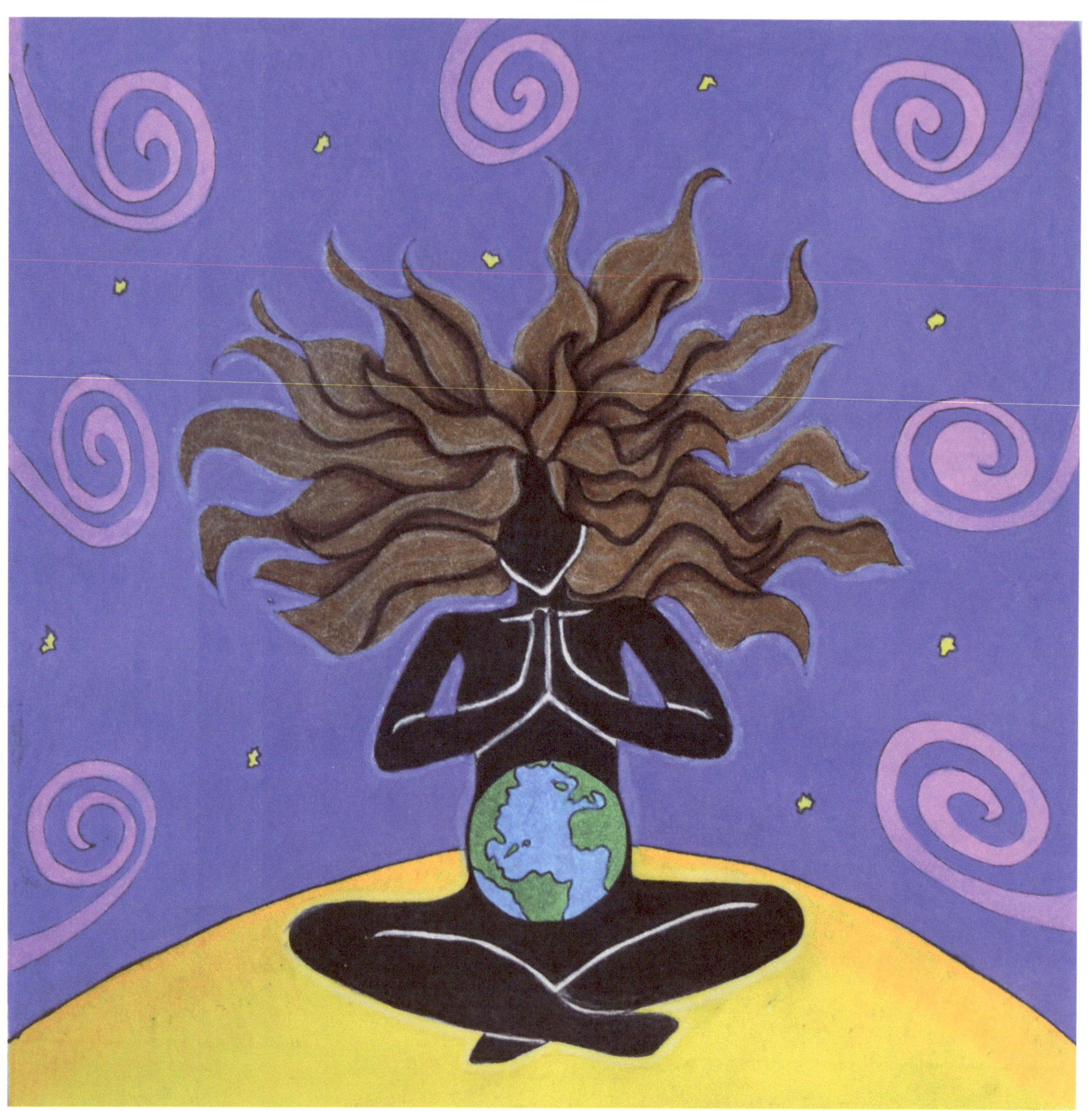

She possesses the right to

CREATE LIFE!

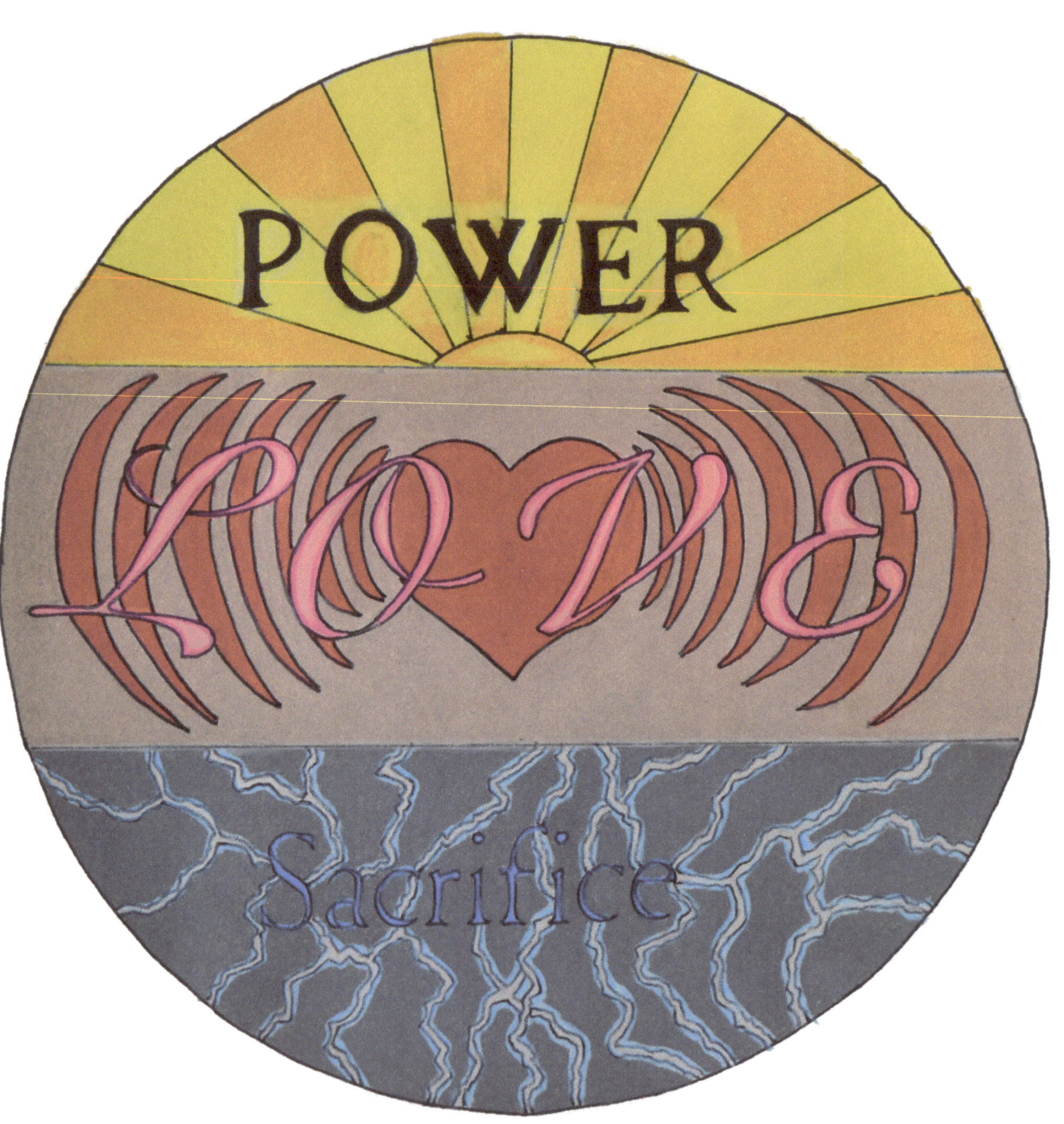
POWER
LOVE
Sacrifice

There is no greater power

There is no greater expression of love

There is no greater sacrifice

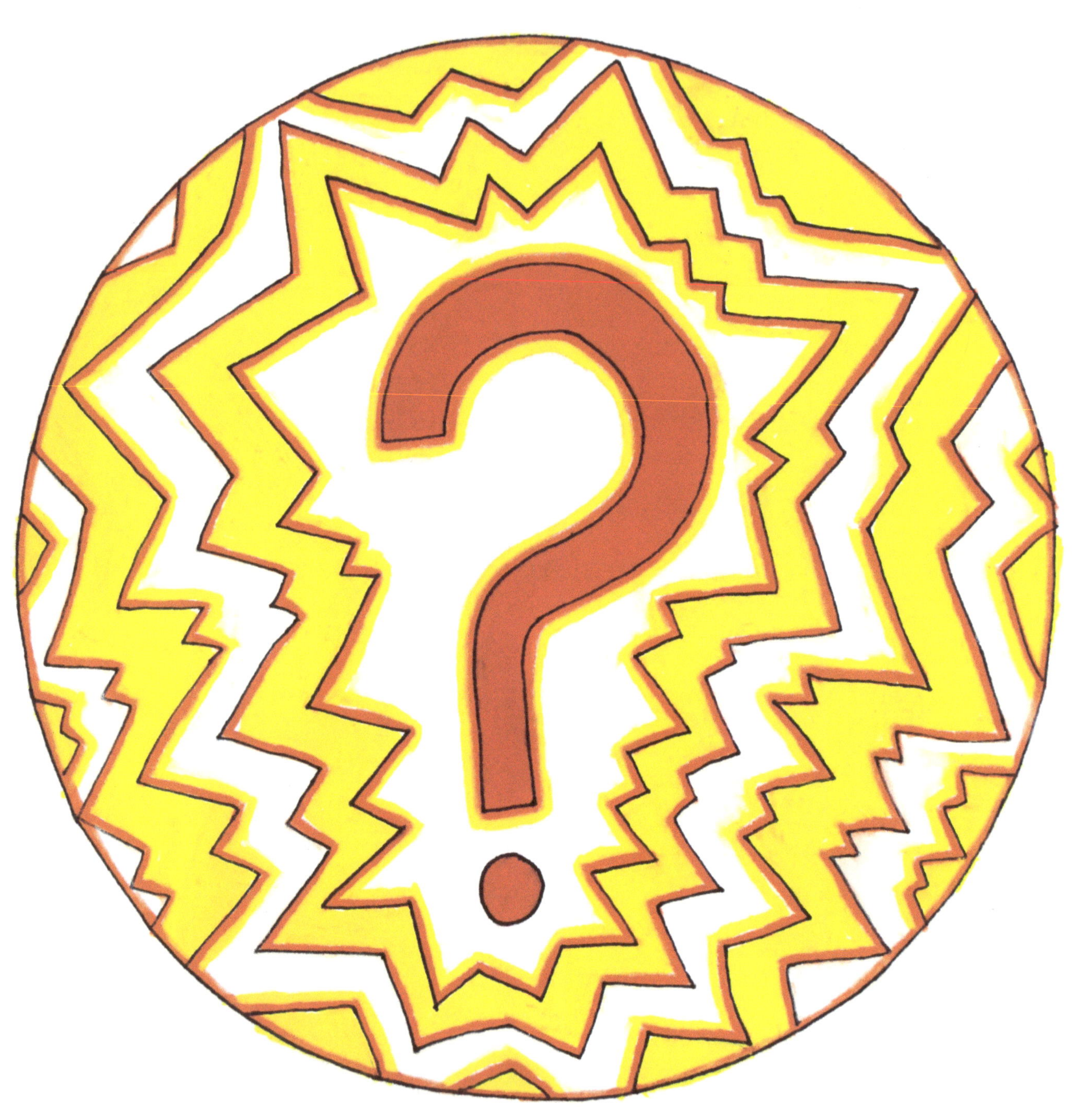

...Or is there?

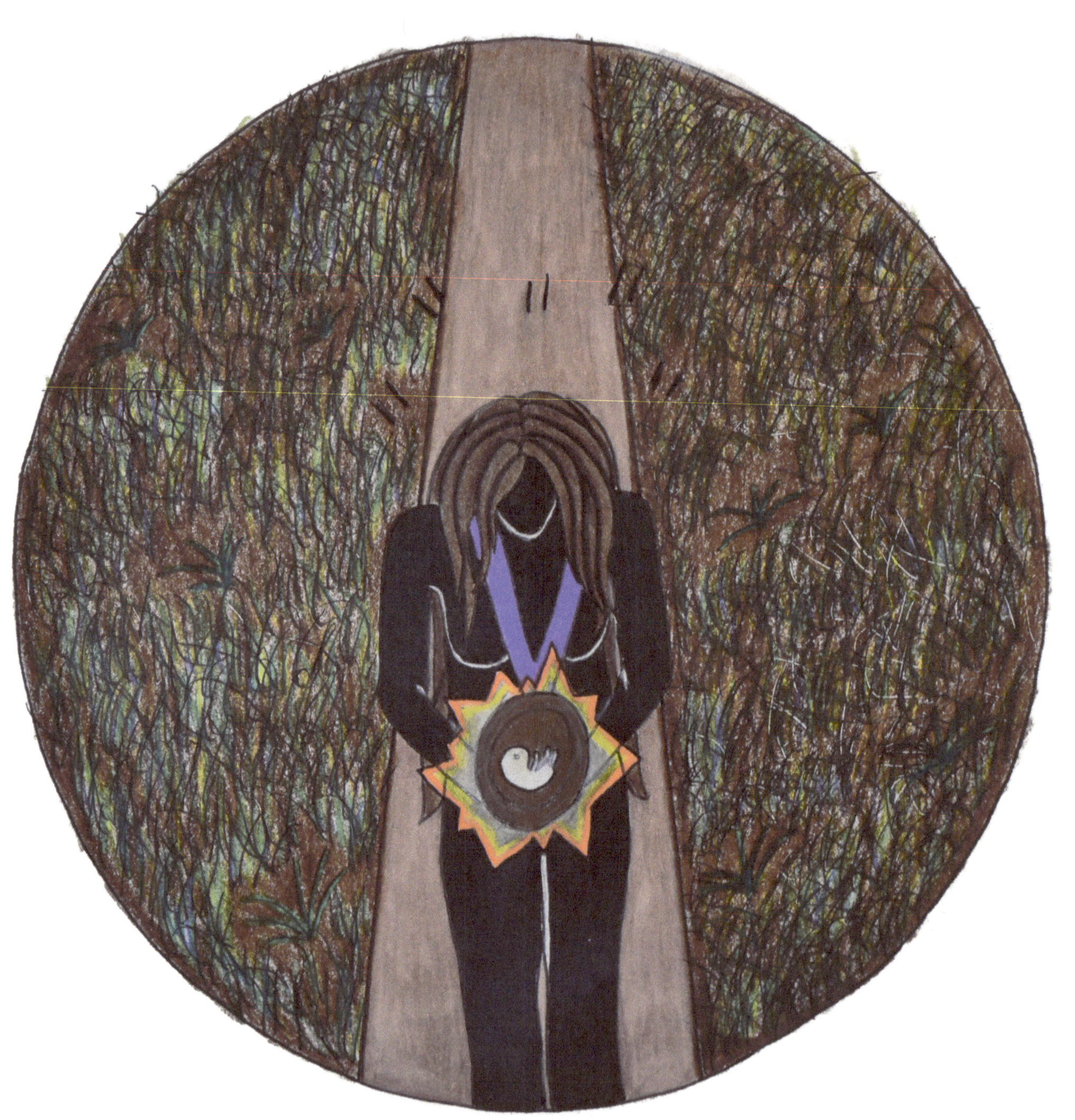

Unsure, but humbled,
She touches her belly
Full of life, of energy, of light

Glowing with the ultimate symbol of Their love

Like a gold medal won
for making it through the human-race

Well deserved for just being Her

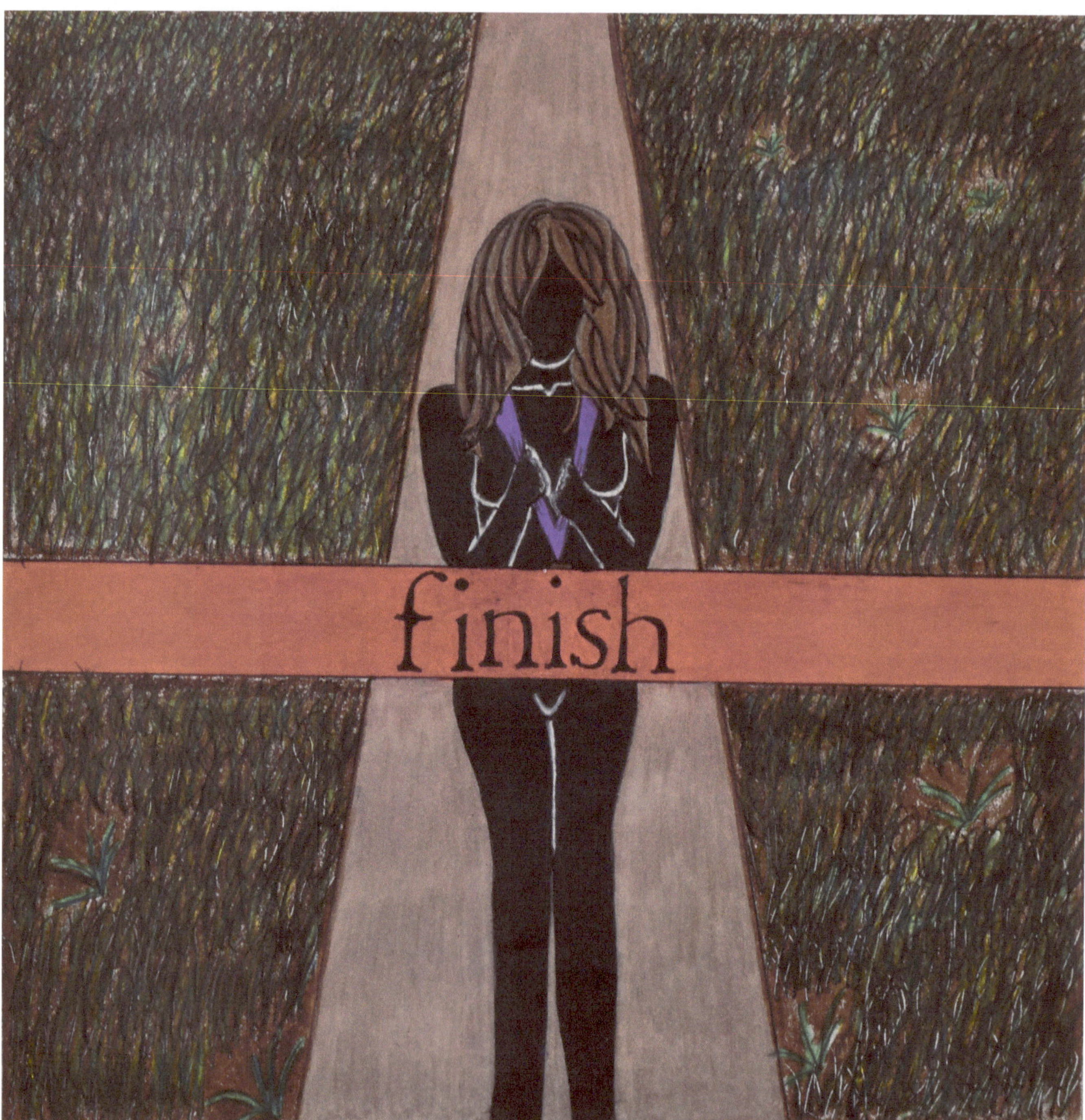
finish

Except,

She hasn't quite crossed the finish line yet.

And reality

sinks

in.

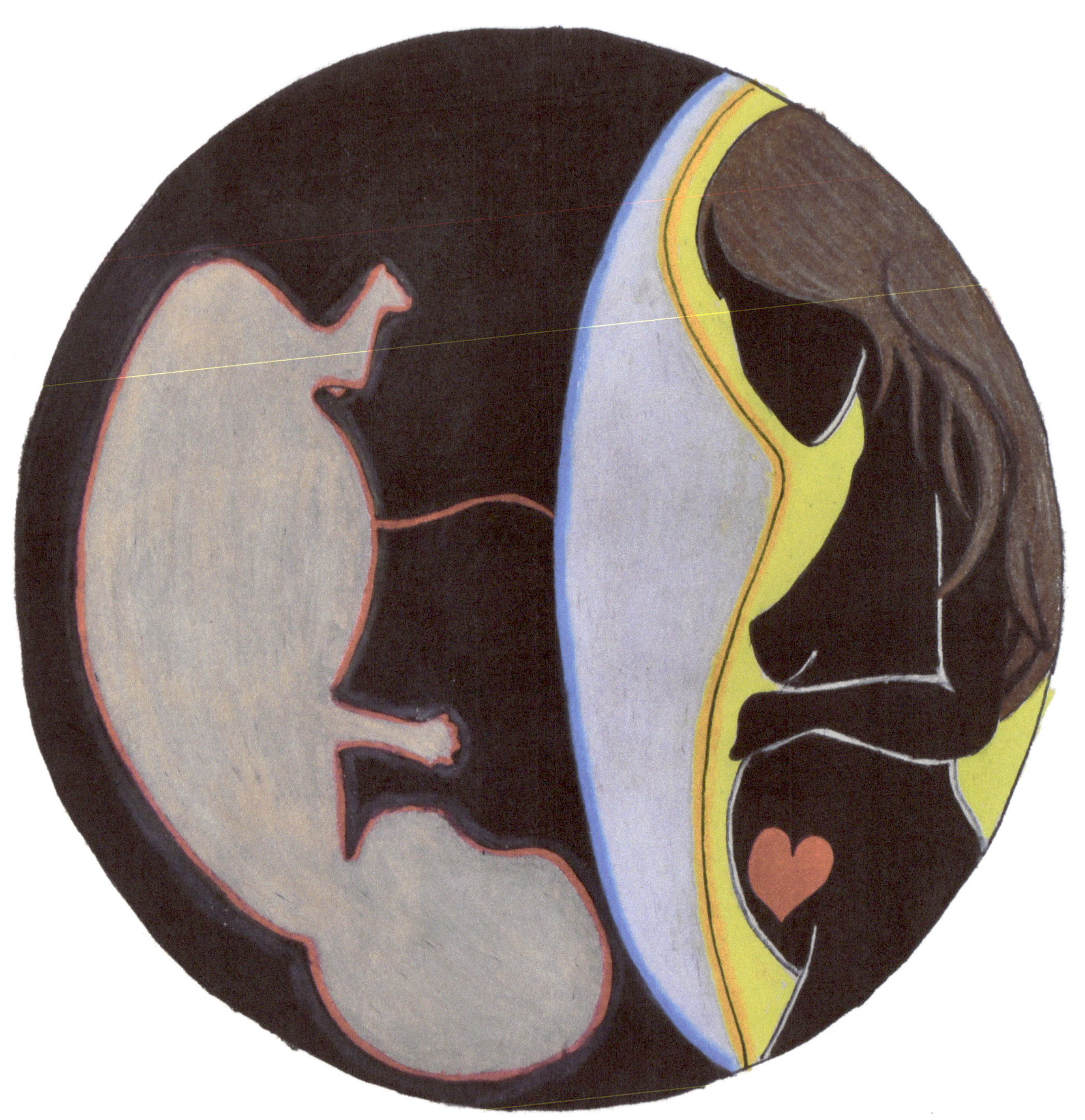

The power to create and destroy life
lay in Her hands.

Lay in between Her legs.

A place so beautiful, so endless
A place so exquisite it makes grown men cry
A place that bleeds red with life…
A place that can bleed red with death,

so She chooses

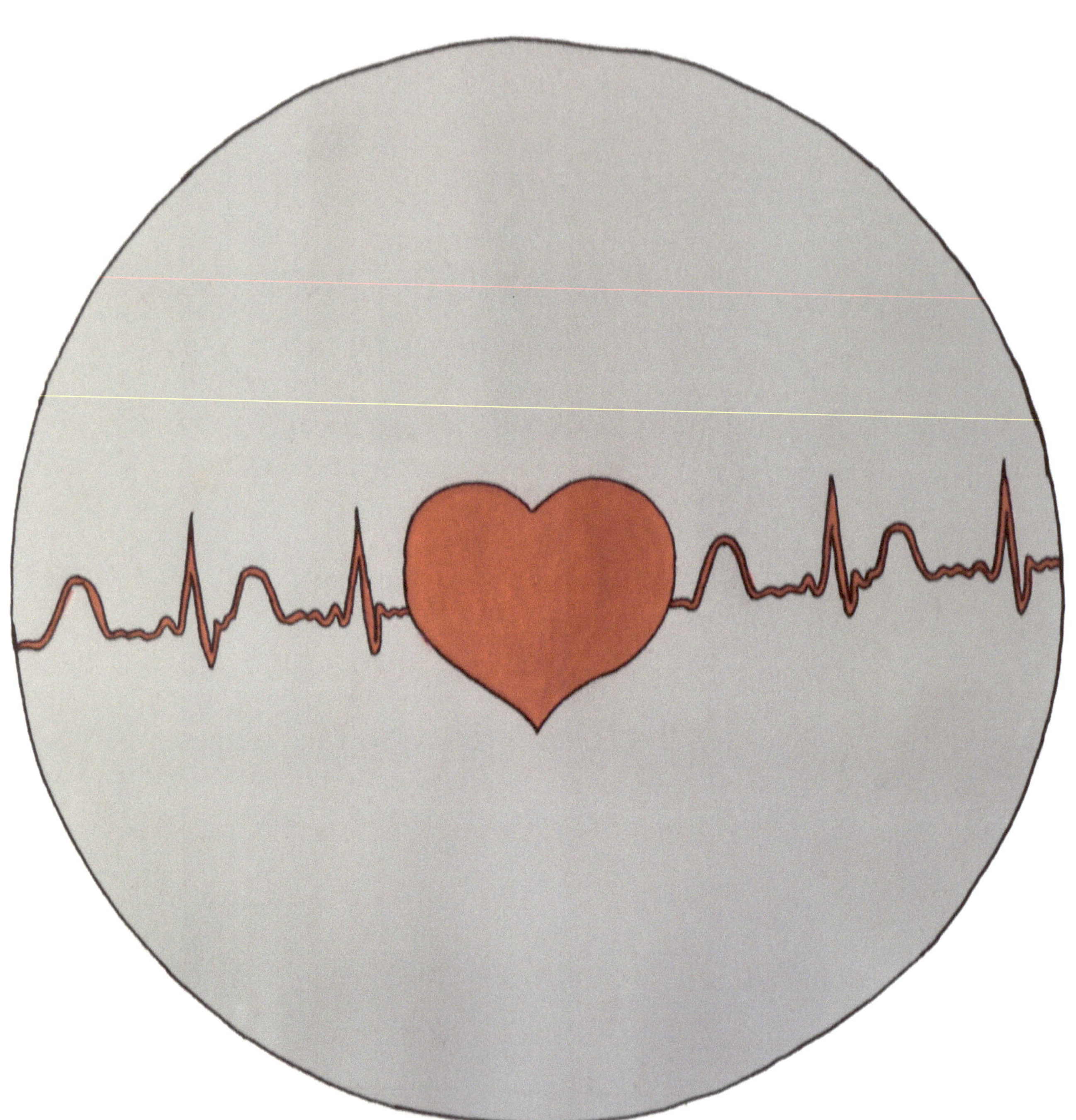

So,

...She chooses...

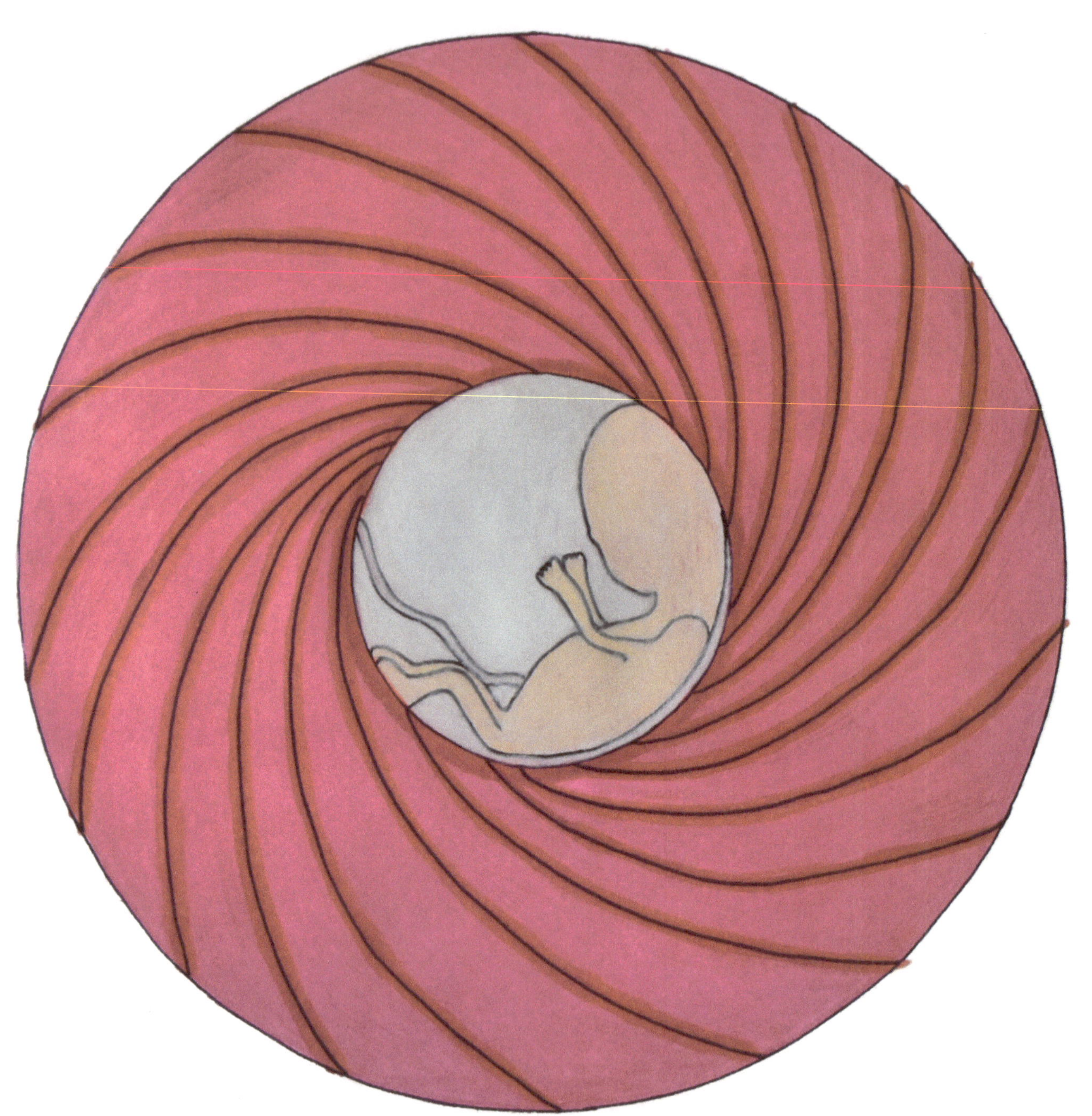

Like looking down the barrel of Heaven's
shotgun given to Her by God Himself

Pointed at the one She loves the most

Allowing Her to decide whether they get a
chance at life or not

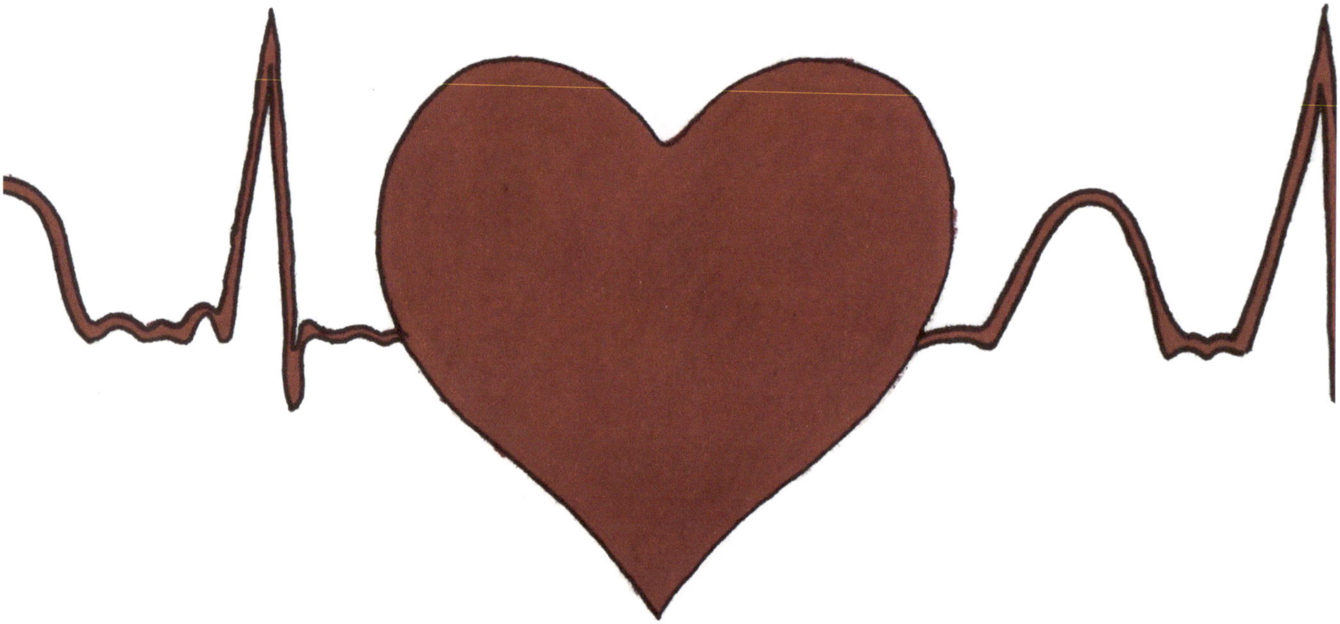

...She chooses...

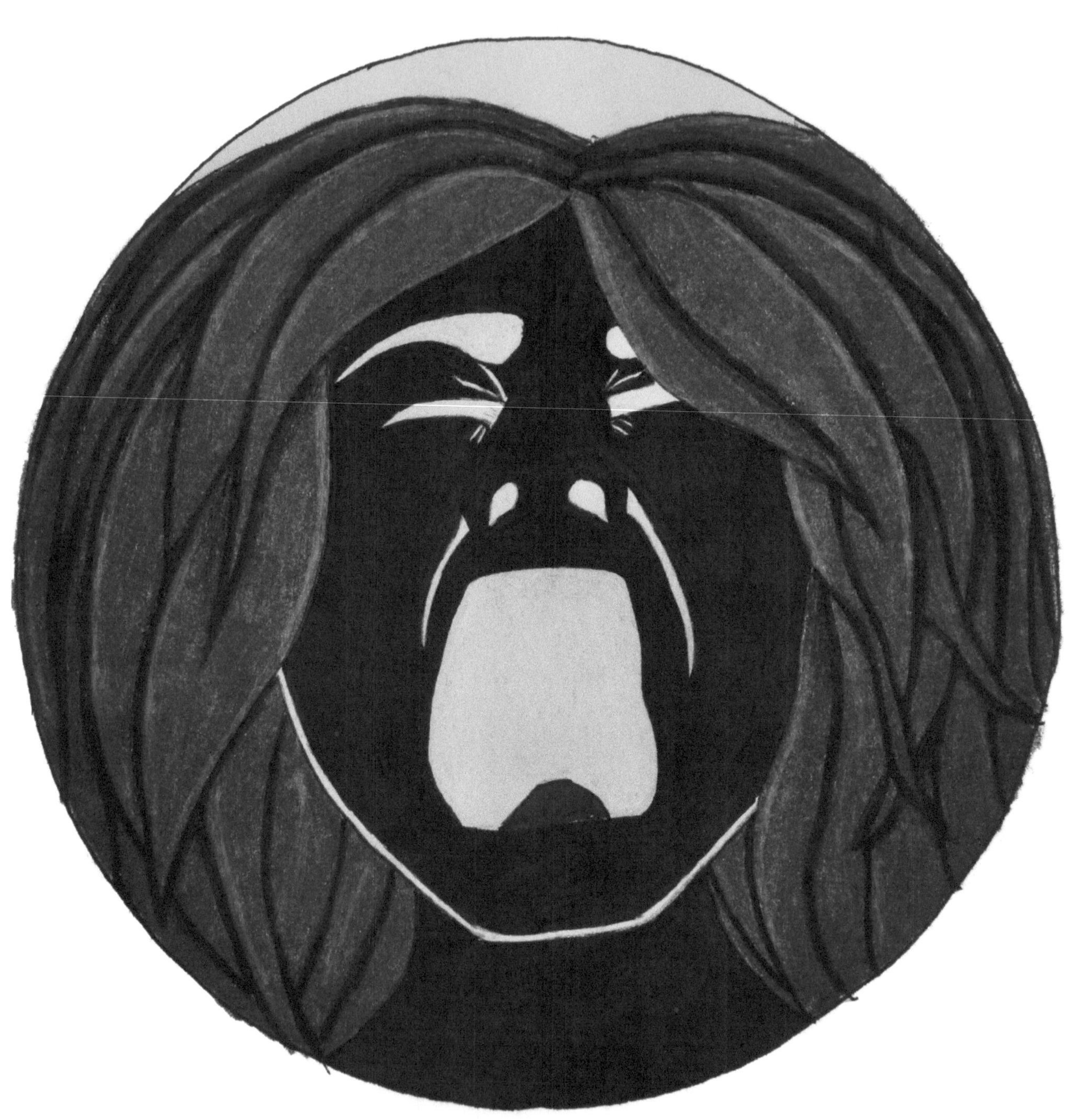

Sacrificing Her self-worth as a woman

Wondering as She screams in terror

How She ever did this the first time

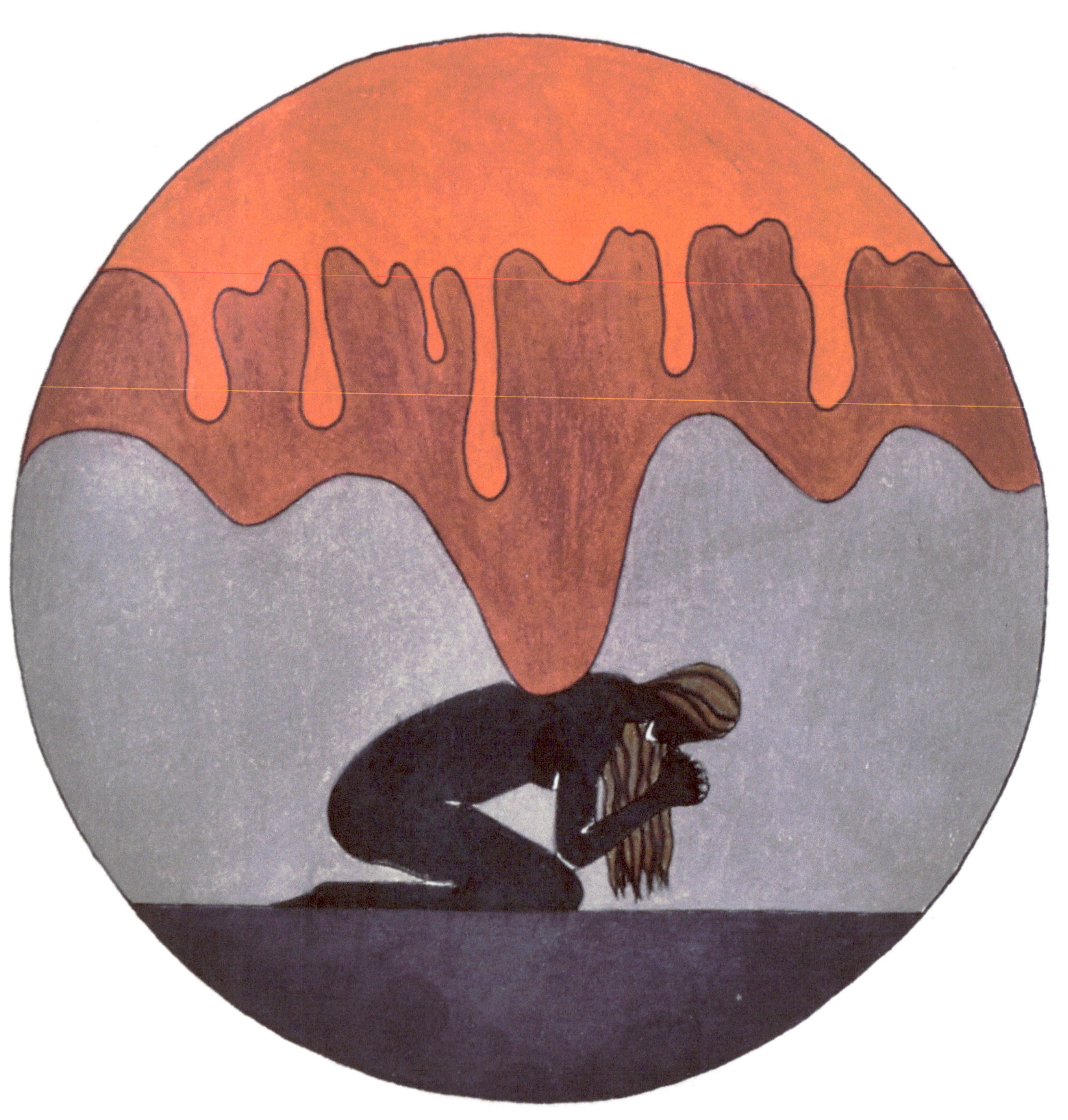

Crying and bleeding for anyone who has ever had life ripped out of them

...She chooses...

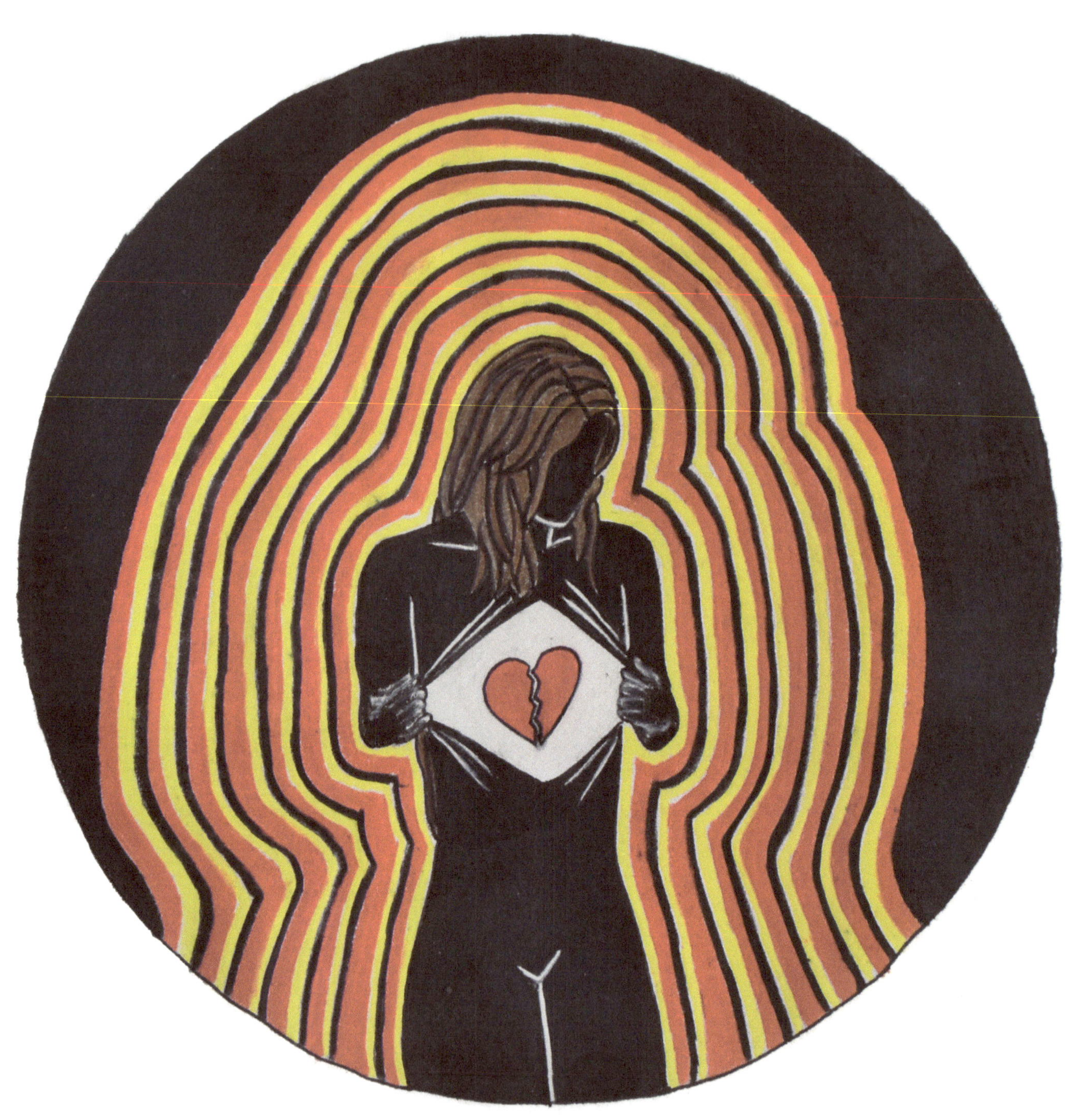

Aware of the repercussions
Her body and soul might endure,

Aware of this gift, this power, this curse

...She chooses...

Like pressing the little red button
that could blow up the world

...She chooses...

BOO

OM!!!

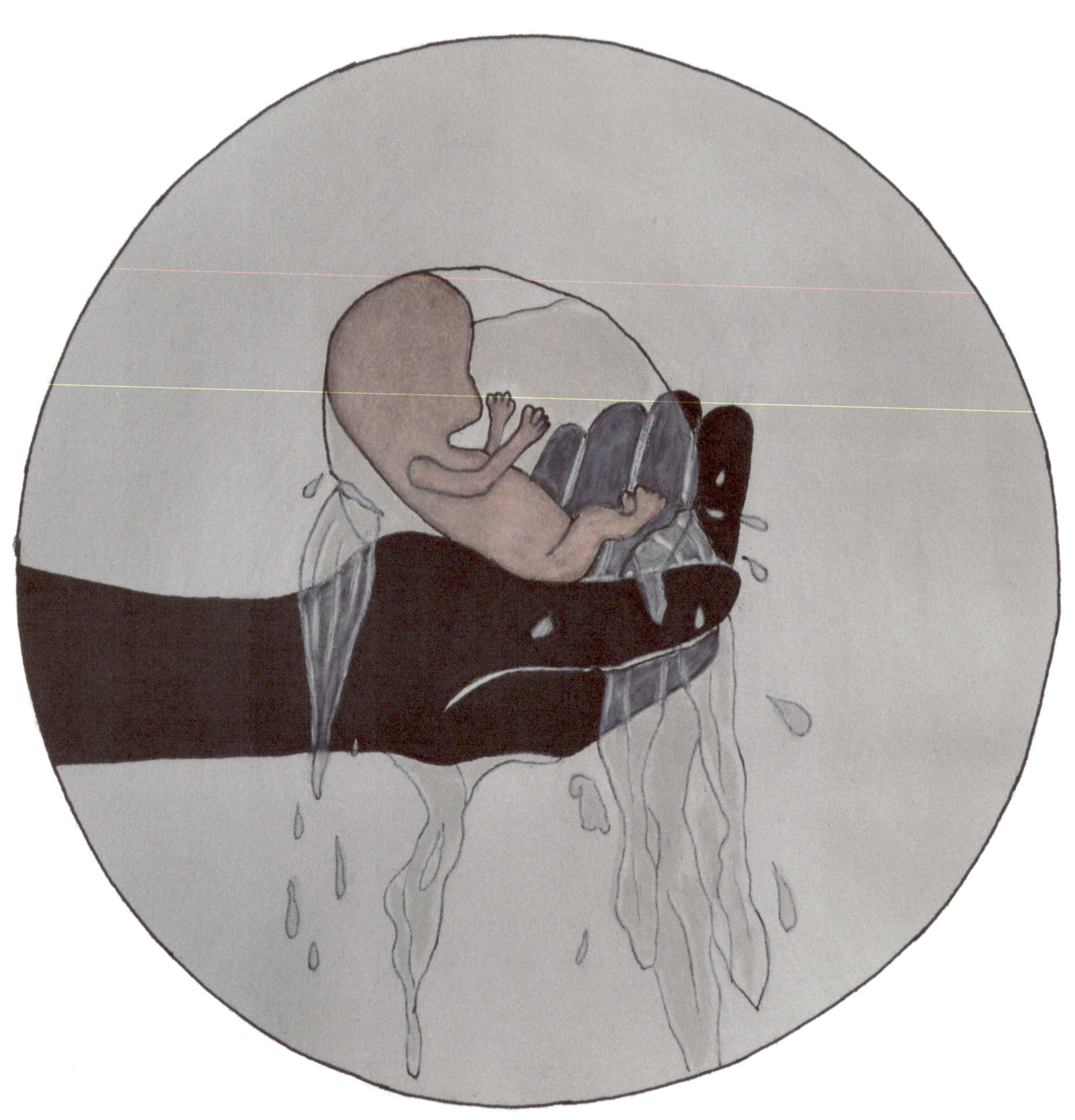

And what took lifetimes of experience,

Years of love making,

And four weeks of the most
complex biochemical reactions

Is gone in a matter of seconds...

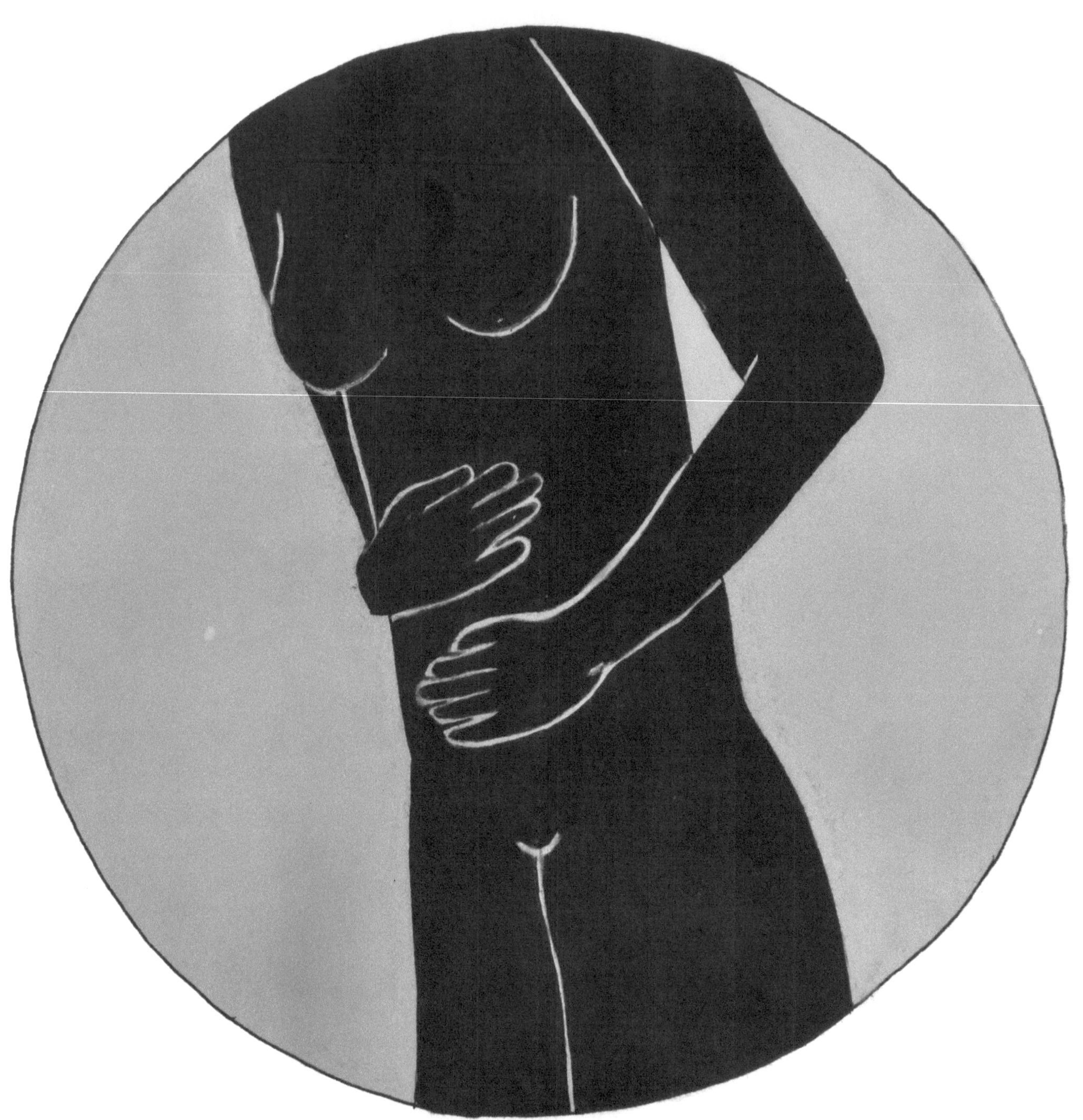

She touches her belly

Silent. Empty.

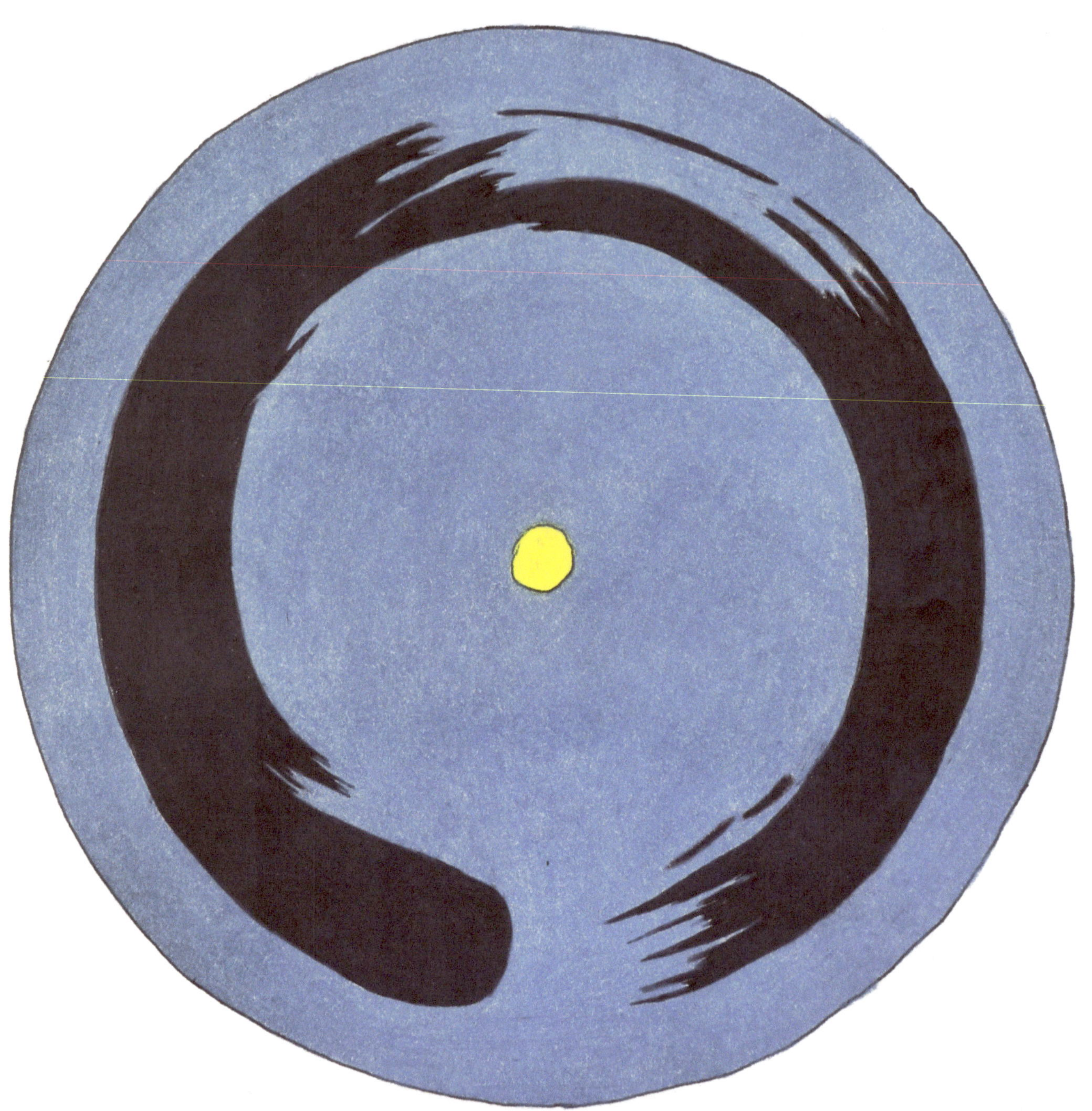

What once was light is now dull.

Not dark,

dull.

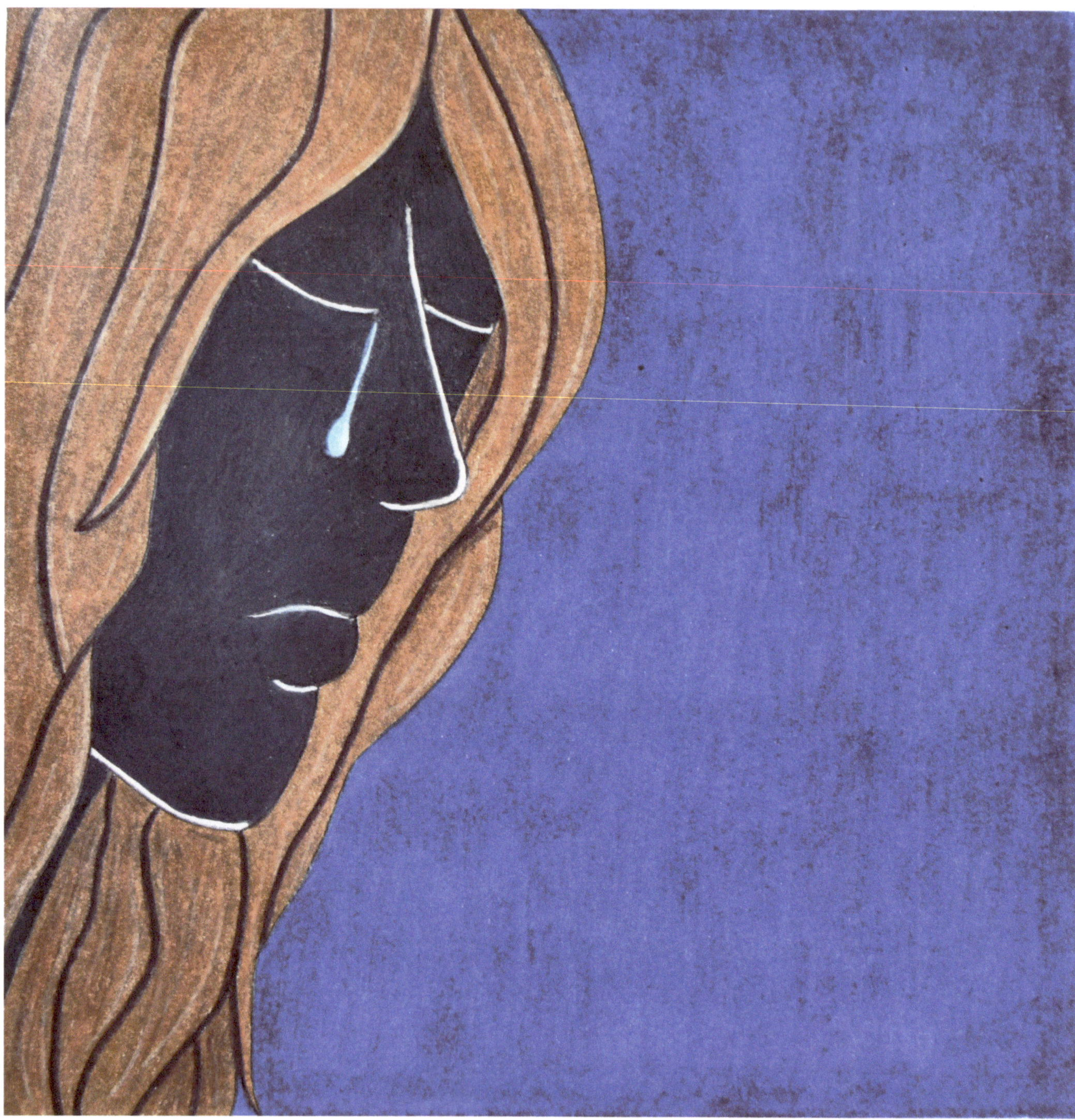

Because that tarnished hint of light
Is so much more painful to feel
She'd rather be blinded, numbed by dark

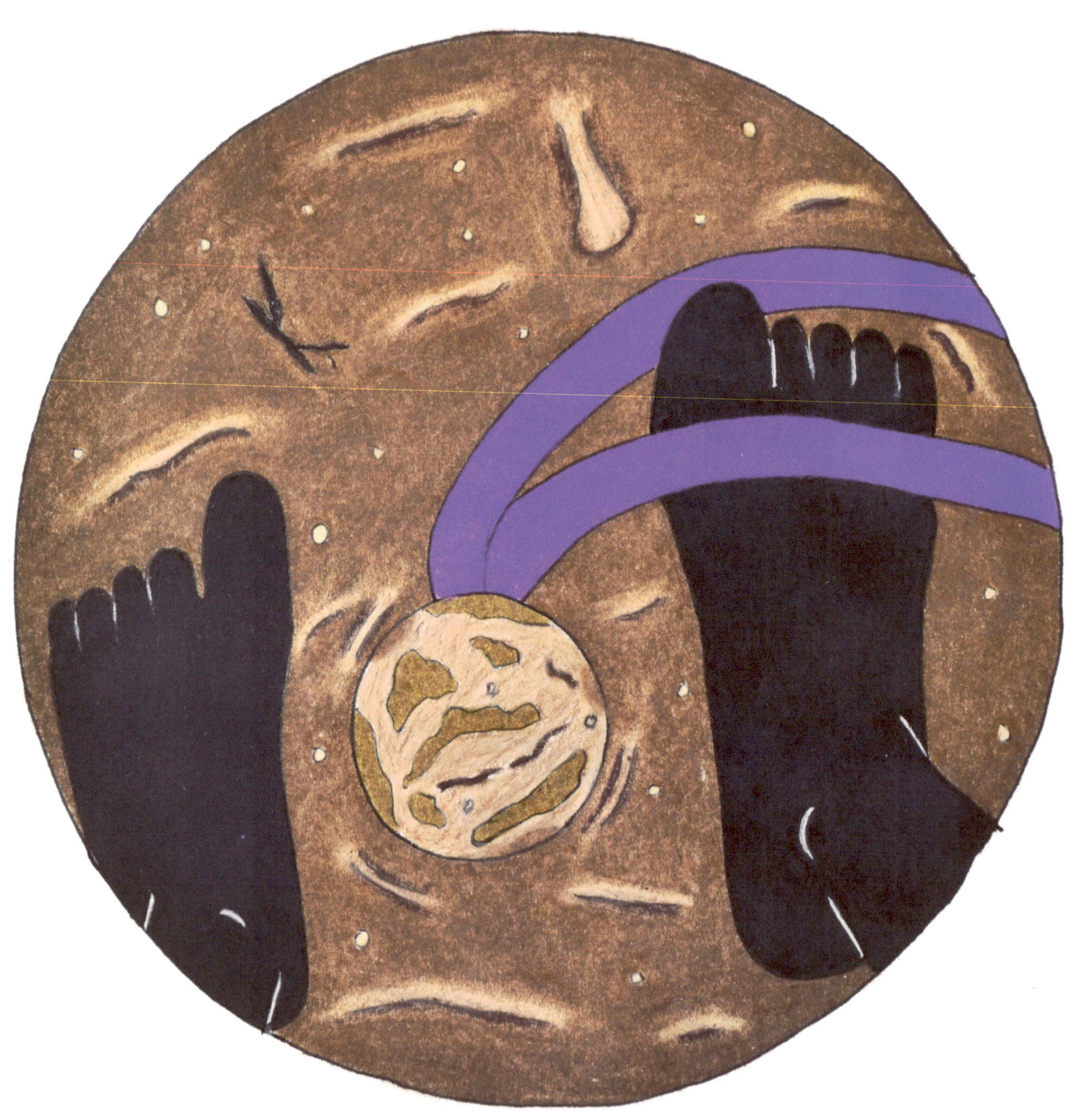

What felt like a gold medal
Now feels like last place

Bronze.

Dirty.

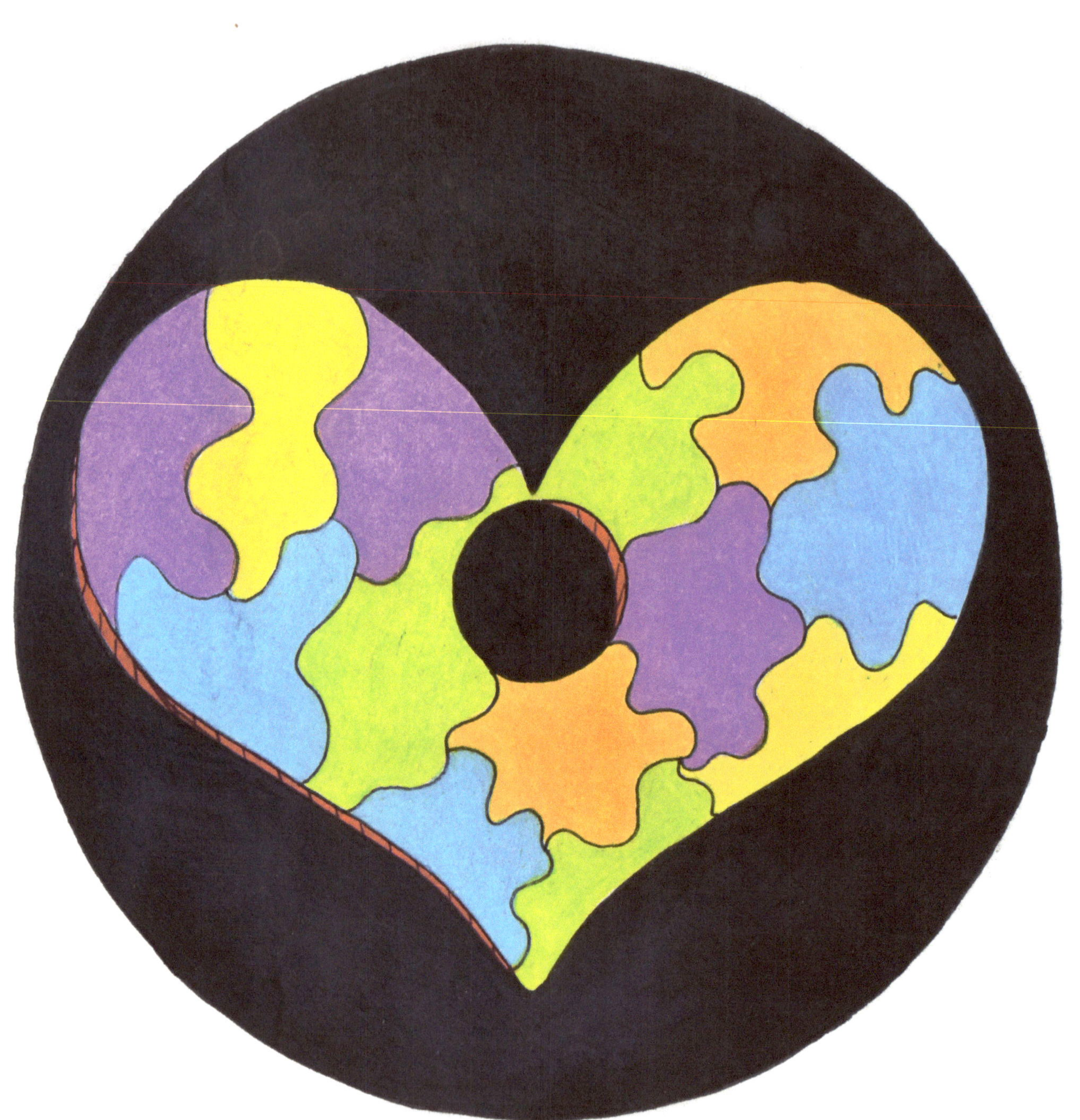

No heartbreak

No death of a loved one

No personal failure

Will ever compare to this void
in a woman's being.

A feeling so profound
words will do it no justice.

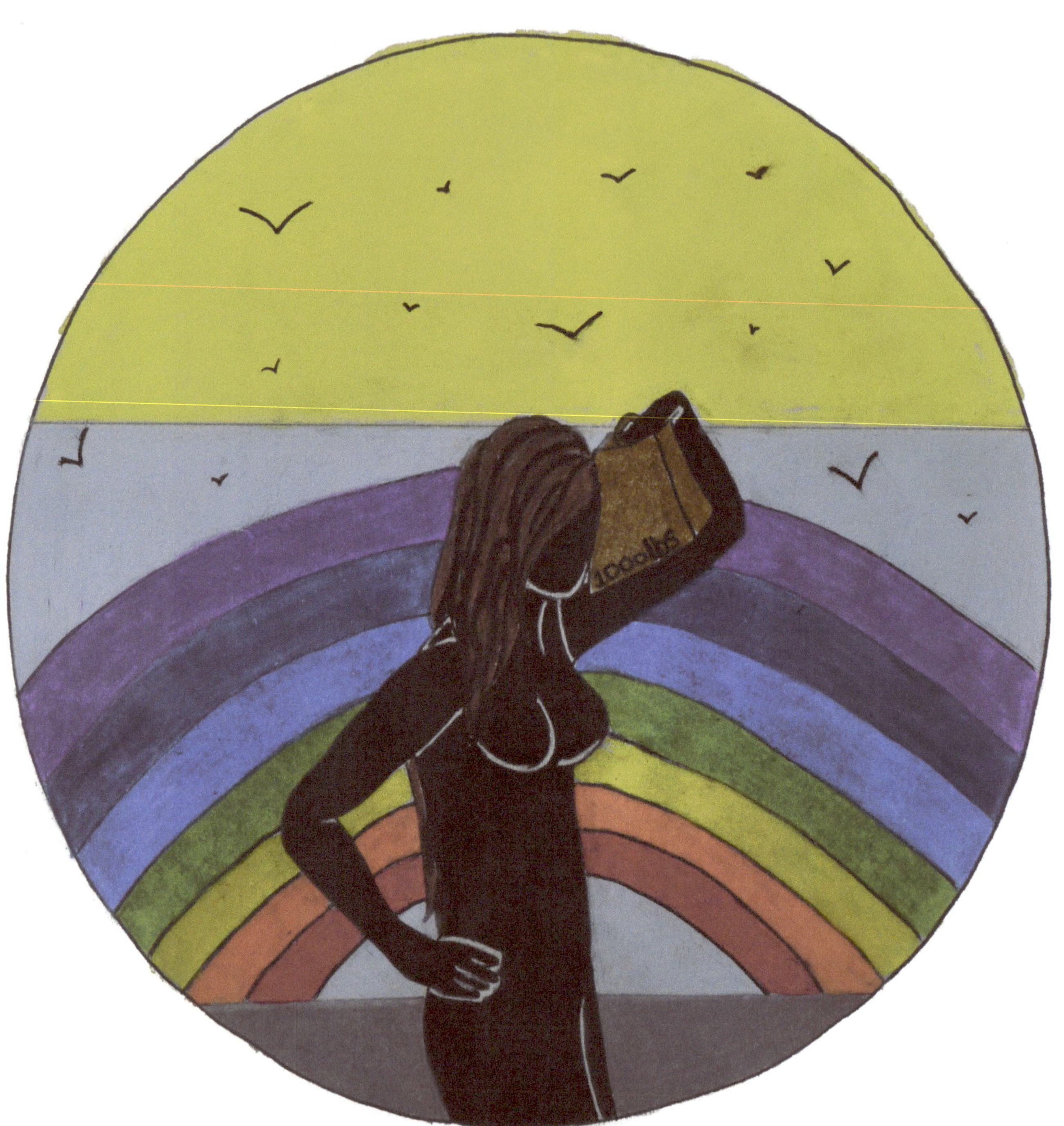
1000lbs

And so She walks around head high

Living life, laughing, going on

Business as usual

Carrying around what She's done...

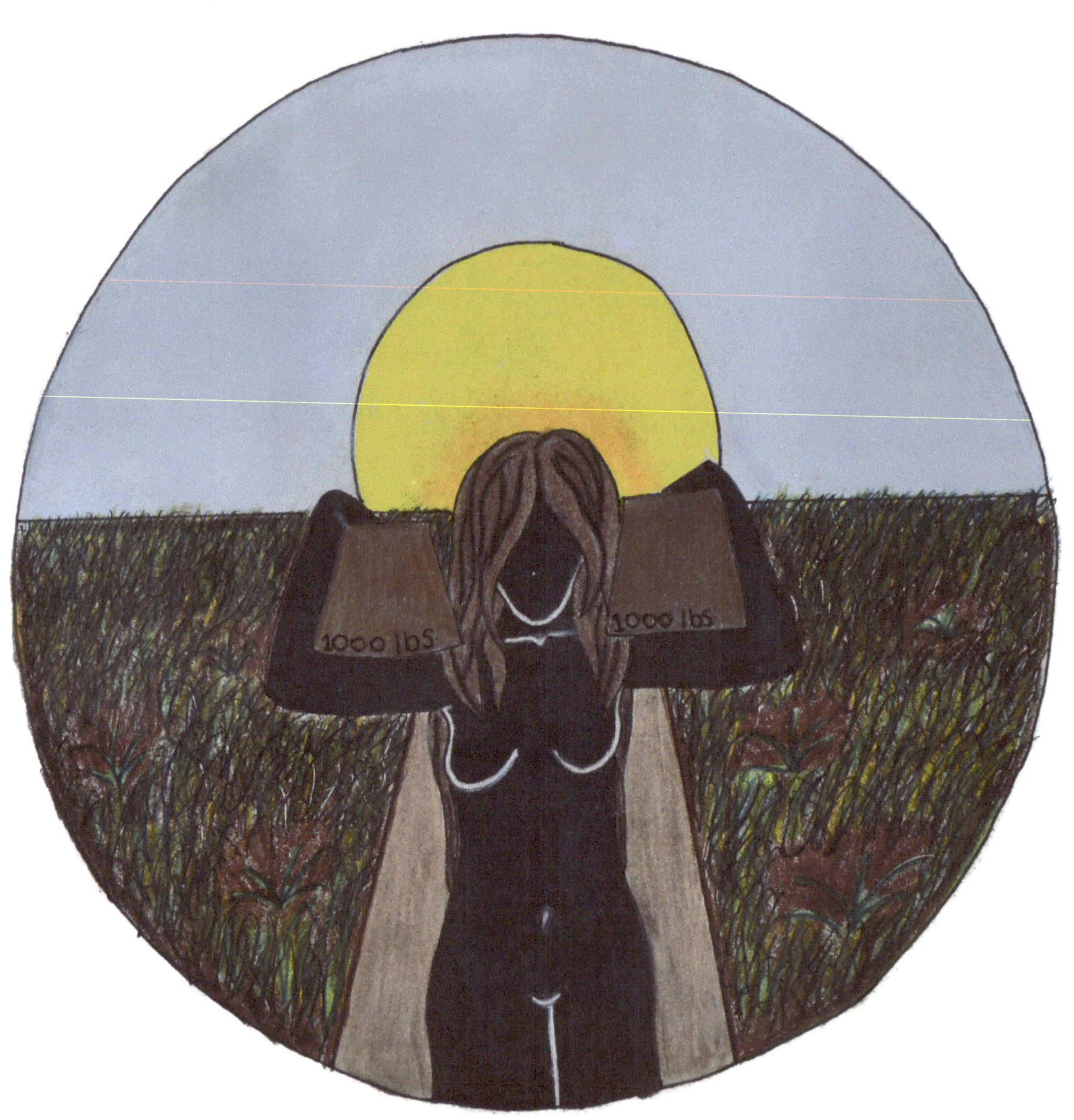
1000 lbs
1000 lbs

...more than once.

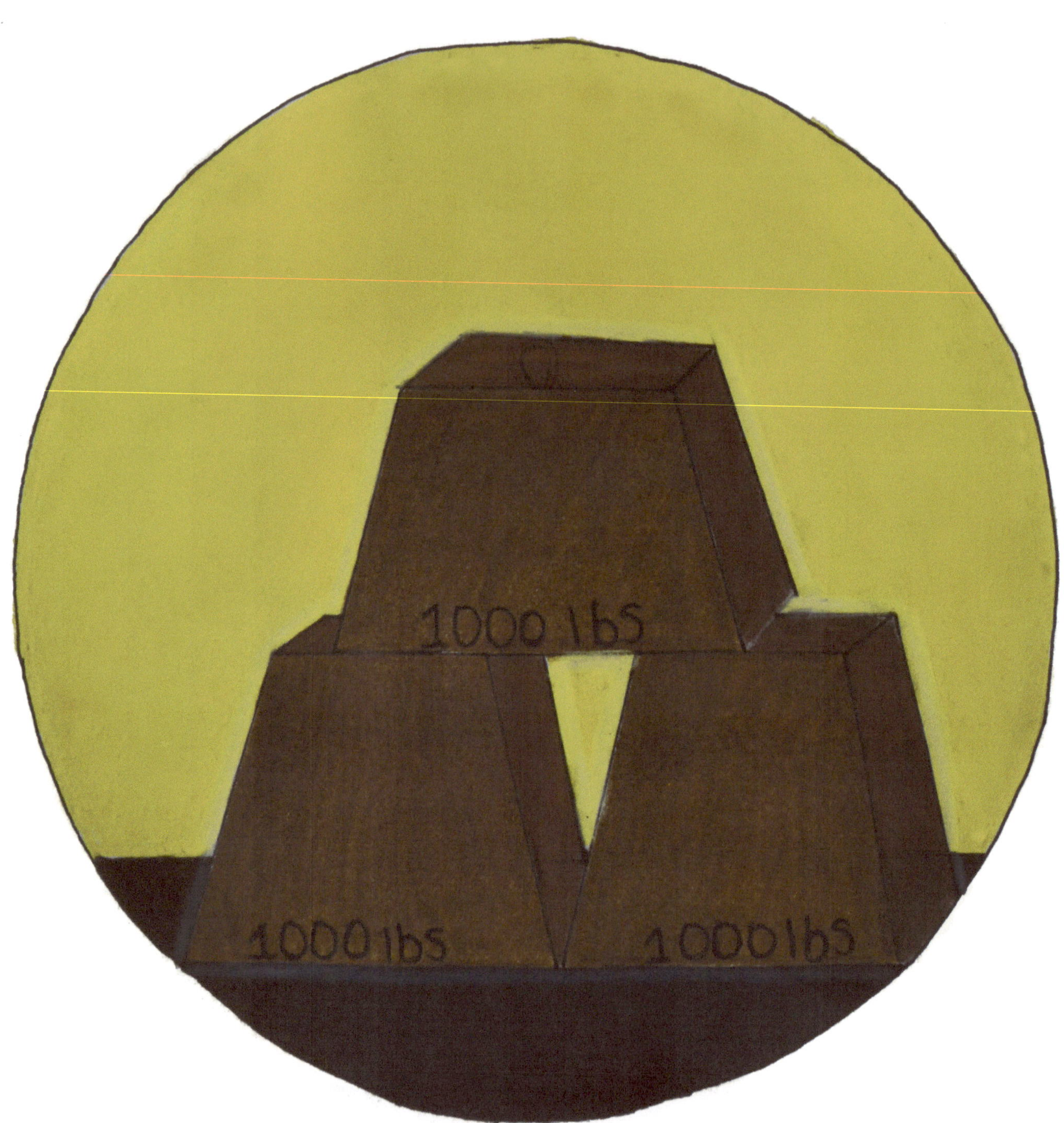
1000 lbs
1000 lbs
1000 lbs

That is Her greatest punishment.

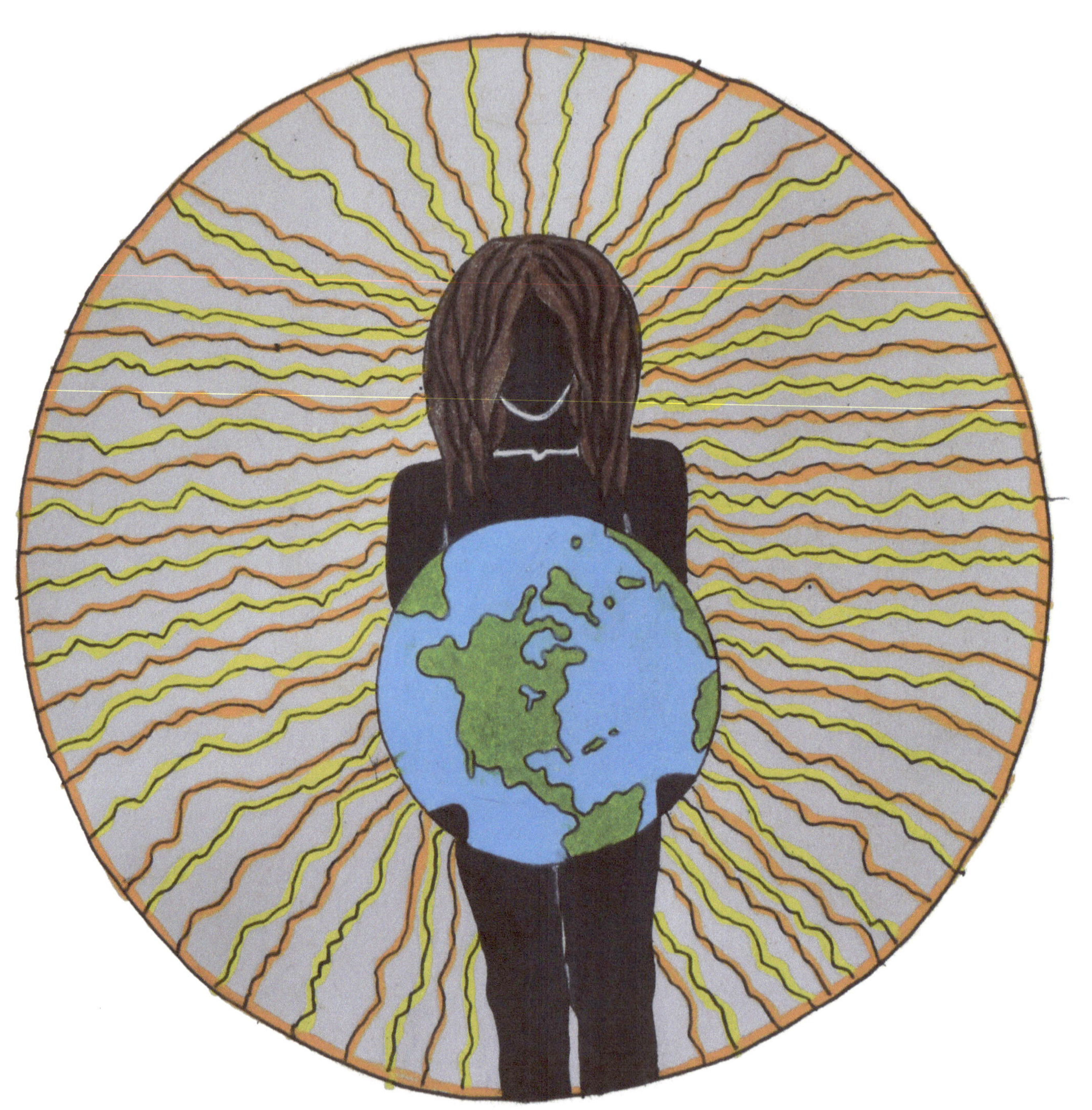

That is the karma of this woman.

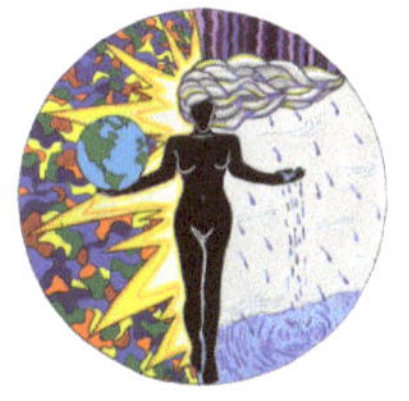

A Note from the Author

Irresponsible! Slut! Baby Killer! You're going to hell!

Oh, hey! Don't mind her. That's just my subconscious thinking out loud. She does that a lot, actually.

Whore! What are you thinking telling the whole world its okay to have an abortion?!

Hey, now wait just one second! I'm not saying it's okay. I'm saying it *will* be okay. Besides, nobody asked you (I say to her).

* * *

New Year's Day, 2002, Brooklyn, New York. Hung over. But at 19, hangovers are easily forgotten throughout the day, masked by more important things like, "What are we gonna do today, guys?" or "Oh, my God, did you see what she was wearing last night?" and "Let's go. You got gas money?" But today's hangover would not bring about such distractions. Today would go more like: "I feel weird, but not like hangover weird. Like weird-weird. Let's stop at the pharmacy. I wanna take a pregnancy test, just in case."

Positive.

"Are you sure?"

Positive.

"Take another one. There's two in the pack."

Positive.

Nobody told me at 19 I'd have to decide between being a mother or chalking another fake ID. Nobody told me that this guy I was with would eventually pull a disappearing act from my life and rip my heart out of my chest. Nobody told me that in a few weeks after the fresh start of a new year, I would experience something that there is just no coming back from.

It's almost like they want to punish you. The nurse shows you the sonogram of this tiny little pebble before they prep you for your "procedure." The image of what it is, and what it one day could be, is permanently imprinted on your soul. As you're rolled into the operating room, and strapped to the bed with your arms out like Jesus being nailed to the cross, the voices and faces in the room become jumbled. It is bright, it is cold. You are shaking, crying, and imagining what your life would look like if you just shouted, "I changed my mind!" What would your poor mother sitting in the waiting room do if you came running out like a mad woman? Would she still have to pay these people? What would this kid look like anyway? Did you shave today?

Then, just as you think you've convinced yourself you're going to leap off the table dramatically and rip the anesthesia IV out of your arm, you hear, "Okay sweetheart, count backwards from 10."

10, 9, 8... *I hope you've learned your lesson!!*

* * *

Summer 2008. Brooklyn, New York. Trips to Jamaica, Vegas, oh, and the plane I never woke up to catch for Puerto Rico because I was too busy celebrating my birthday the night before. I had my life together like any other single 26-year-old girl sleeping with a man who already had children. *Home wrecker!!* But, in my defense, my biological clock was ticking. Besides, he made love to me like the fate of all humanity depended on it. I was completely drenched in our escapades; stuck in that space between reality and not giving a fuck about consequences of any actions taken.

Whore!!

And before I knew it, as any self-fulfilling prophecy goes, I ended up getting what I had secretly hoped for. He would be so happy! He loves me. We can make it work. So what if he just had his second child a year ago?

And just like that, a few disappointing encounters and conversations later, "we" decided maybe it was not such a great idea after all. No big deal, I suppose. I've done it before and survived. I can get through it again. He was nice enough to come with me. The nurses here just loaded me up on Valium and told me to try and stay still. I'd be awake and have a front row seat to this ungodly act which I would have to endure for five minutes or so while Alicia Keys' song "Karma" played on the radio in the background.

Karma!!

I had come full circle. Right back to where I had been seven years ago, and I had a theme song to go with it.

"What goes around comes around, what goes up must come down..."

* * *

I wrote the poem in this book at 26 years old, after my second experience with pregnancy. My purpose with this book is neither to promote nor condemn abortion. It is not to argue what is right or wrong. It is a channel for others to tune into for support. It is to help give a voice to the unexplainable emotions a woman goes through during such a difficult time in her life. It is to bring awareness to such a taboo subject. It is also to stir the pot. To make those who believe it is sin uncomfortable in order for them to face their own fears. It is to help create empathy and more understanding towards others' personal decisions. Most importantly, it is for me. To move forward. To forgive myself. To forgive the men in my life. To live out my karma.

ଓ

Acknowledgements

I could not begin without acknowledging the courage of my baby blue sisters, Soltier and Michelle, to take this poem I wrote ages ago and bring it back to life. It is because of you ladies that I took a leap of faith and decided to bring this to a wider audience. Thank you for reminding me I am not alone, we are not alone.

To my publisher, Cynthia Ceilán, for taking a chance on someone she's never met. Your work ethic and positive attitude has made this scary journey a whole lot easier.

To my late father, Terrence J. Pierson. You always taught me to push and go further. You encouraged me to write at a very young age, and one of your dying wishes was to hear my poetry. I'm sorry I was too embarrassed to share any of my work with you. Regardless the topic of my story, I know you are proud of me and this accomplishment. You always loved me no matter what. Thank you, Daddy!

The two first and most important women in my life and the most headstrong females I've ever known, my mother, Carmen, and my sister, Miriela. You both raised me and helped shape me into what I am today, and although the road has been a bumpy one at times, I am grateful. You may not understand or agree with some of my crazy, but I know through it all I can always count on you for support and protection. Thank you!

Kimberly Febo. What can I say? We've got something really special going here. Your art and my words were meant to be. I really think you're secretly from another planet because what you have in your heart and what you do for this world is just beyond comprehension. I am so proud of you. Your work affirms to the rest of the world that you can do anything you put your love into, against any and all odds.

To my best friend and partner, Dennis Febo, without whom I would not have my three beautiful children. You are my mentor and my inspiration. Your fearlessness is everything I need when I'm scared. You've taught me to live without limits and through the ups and downs we remain a strong unit.

My sons, Cayden and Julian, your unconditional love helps me strive to be the best person I can be. I pray that one day you learn to love your partner as pure and true as the way you love your Mommy.

And finally, to my one and only little girl, Amayah Devi. My heart breaks and I lose a small piece of my sanity every time I sit and ponder your future as a woman in this world. There will be so many obstacles, especially for you, my sweet girl. But you are strong and resilient. May your will carry you through any and every experience you face. I pray you make better judgment calls than I ever did, and that you will never have to face a decision like this in your life.

—Barbara Pierson

I would like to humbly acknowledge my mother Clarabelle James, who was my first example of a woman. She taught me unconditional love through her example of love for us and those around her. She taught me how to smile and be grateful through dark and light times, and also how to make the best of any situation. My father, Osvaldo Febo, for teaching me how to have a sense of humor by not taking things so seriously, and finding light and positivity no matter the situation. He taught me how to let go of the past and appreciate what is in front of me in every moment. To my grandmother Isabel Santiago, for sparking creativity in me in my very early years, and teaching me that I can create anything I wanted to as long as I applied myself and was patient. To my grandfather Jose Santiago, who was my main example for taking care of those things and people that meant the world to me and never to turn my back on any of it, no matter what I am going through.

I would like extend profound gratitude to my brothers Dennis Febo, Stephen Febo, Hector Rosado, Kamal James, Derek Henry, and Jose Sanchez for being the greatest example of what a gentlemen truly is, and for being the example of the man every woman should have standing by her side. Thank you for always uplifting the women around you and for believing in me, even when I did not. You all pushed me through words and example, and all of your strengths pushed away all of my fears and helped shine light on why I have to continue doing the work that I am setting out to do. To my sister Rebecca Rosado for being such a bright light in my life and giving me hope, through who you are, that I can make my future bright and for showing me through example that I can be as strong, fearless, and loving as I want to be, because it is something that I own, I was born with, and no one can take away from me, if I know it and believe it.

I would like to honor my soul sisters Lorean Valentin, Monica DelaCruz, Lizbeth Felix, Barbara Pierson, Amarilis Sanchez, Yarilis Sanchez, Estee Abreu, Rochelle Breton, and Judy Brown. You all, through thick and thin, good and bad, have been perfect examples of the woman I want to amount to be. You have been a light upon my path of strength, comfort, support, wisdom, and the essence of the true power that lies within all of us women. Thank you for being such a great support and source of incredible example in my life. Thank you for lighting my spirit when all I saw was darkness, and thank you for pushing me even when I saw the way.

I wish to express my deep affection and appreciation to my husband Hector Breton. You are the reason I am today. Thank you for lighting my way and teaching me to believe in me. You are the air that I breathe. To my children Jayden, Anthony and Lailah, thank you for giving me purpose. I look at you and see hope for your future. You are the light of my life.

My deepest and sincerest gratitude to my dearest Cynthia Ceilán. You have been such a positive support system and light throughout this journey. Thank you for giving me such a beautiful opportunity. There are no words that could ever express the gratitude I feel for having the opportunity to have been able to work with such a beautiful soul.

—Kimberly Febo

About the Author

Barbara Pierson is a native of Brooklyn, New York, who is now raising a beautiful family with her husband in New Jersey. At a very young age, Barbara realized that she enjoyed rhyming words together to make up stories. Thus began a long journey of learning to express her feelings through writing and creativity.

Throughout her college years, Barbara took part in advanced writing courses and attended many spoken-word performances to help sharpen her craft. *The Karma of a Woman* has been used as a performance piece in various venues throughout New York.

As of late, Barbara's work focuses mainly on issues that affect women. She aspires to be a voice for those women who have encountered situations that are very personal and may be difficult to cope with.

About the Illustrator

Kimberly Febo is a native of Brooklyn, New York, raised in many different parts of the United States and Puerto Rico. She is an artist, singer, and writer whose work focuses on inspiring strength, love, peace, and uplifting the spirit through freedom of creative expression. While growing up in such diverse communities, she was exposed to many different backgrounds, cultures, and realities, allowing her to see things through many different perspectives. Through these experiences, she gained the gift of clarity, and the ability to speak knowledge to people from many different points of view, giving them the clarity and uplifting they need at any given moment.

She has worked as a children's and youth leader in her community, and has counseled hundreds of people of all age groups and family members throughout her lifetime with her singing, artwork, and spoken-word performances. Her studio is located in Orlando, Florida, where she resides with her husband and children. Learn more about Kimberly and her work at www.ArtofAwakeningStudio.com.

www.ingramcontent.com/pod-product-compliance
Lightning Source LLC
LaVergne TN
LVHW070509120826
845147LV00031BA/266
* 9 7 8 0 9 9 0 7 7 9 0 3 2 *